ATTEMPT GREAT THINGS FOR GOD

THEOLOGICAL EDUCATION BETWEEN THE TIMES

Ted A. Smith, series editor

Theological Education between the Times gathers diverse groups of people for critical, theological conversations about the meanings and purposes of theological education in a time of deep change. The project is funded by the Lilly Endowment Inc.

Willie James Jennings
After Whiteness: An Education in Belonging

Chloe T. Sun
Attempt Great Things for God: Theological Education in Diaspora

Amos Yong
Renewing the Church by the Spirit: Theological Education after Pentecost

Attempt Great Things for God

Theological Education in Diaspora

Chloe T. Sun

William B. Eerdmans Publishing Company

Grand Rapids, Michigan

Wm. B. Eerdmans Publishing Co.
4035 Park East Court SE, Grand Rapids, Michigan 49546
www.eerdmans.com

Published 2020
Printed in the United States of America

26 25 24 23 22 21 20   1 2 3 4 5 6 7

ISBN 978-0-8028-7842-7

Library of Congress Cataloging-in-Publication Data

Names: Sun, Chloe Tse, author.
Title: Attempt great things for God : theological education in
    disaspora / Chloe T. Sun.
Description: Grand Rapids, Michigan : William B. Eerdmans Publish-
    ing Company, 2020. | Series: Theological education between the
    times | Includes bibliographical references. | Summary: "A case
    study of one Chinese-language seminary in the United States and
    what it has to teach us about theological education in the modern,
    diverse world"—Provided by the publisher.
Identifiers: LCCN 2020023991 | ISBN 9780802878427 (paperback)
Subjects: LCSH: Theology—Study and teaching—History—21st
    century.
Classification: LCC BV4020 .S86 2020 | DDC 230.071/17—dc23
LC record available at https://lccn.loc.gov/2020023991

Contents

v

Introduction

Theological Education in Diaspora

Our era is one of rapid and widespread dispersion of people. Numerous people groups are migrating, relocating, or being displaced from their countries of origin to other parts of the world. It is a time of globalization, of diaspora. But more importantly for Christians, it is a time for the propagation of the gospel. As a Chinese evangelical Christian woman who for over sixteen years has taught in the United States at a Chinese evangelical seminary accredited by the Association of Theological Schools (ATS), I inhabit a peculiar social location. On the one hand, I am a newcomer to the long history of theological education in North America, dwelling at the periphery of the main narratives in the West. On the other hand, I am also at the center of a new wave of energy in theological education in the diaspora.

As the number of immigrants in the United States has increased, and as the number of Christians in Africa, Asia, and Latin America has grown, a new wave is flooding the contemporary landscape of theological education—a wave of students from historically minoritized ethnic groups as well as from current multicultural contexts in various diasporic communities. While Christianity in the West shows signs of general decline, with churches closing and enrollment in many theological schools falling, in the Chinese, Korean, and Hispanic diasporas the numbers of churches, believers, and theological schools are all soaring. Consequently, it is logical to anticipate a future of theological education marked by its global nature, with increasing diversity of cultural demographics within schools, more students from diasporic communities, an expanding number of educational models, and a growing pluralism of theological practices. Christianity's center of gravity has shifted from the minority world to the majority world. Thanks to this shift, I have become both an insider and an outsider of the main narratives. My school and I are participants in and shapers of what Daniel Aleshire, the former ATS executive director, has called the "next future" of theological education.

Three narratives dominate the current and future landscape of theological schools in North America: (1) the decline of the MDiv degree; (2) tensions around slavery and its afterlives that define race in terms of black and white; and (3) struggles around the marginalization of women in ministry and leadership. While each of these narratives is important, even together they are not the whole story. This book tells a previously untold story. It moves to the center a new narrative told by neglected voices that forces both dominant groups and minoritized groups to rethink and reframe the meaning and purpose of theological education between the times. It suggests an alternative future of theological education in the diaspora. Using Logos Evangelical Seminary as a case study, the book argues that the aforementioned three dominant narratives do not resonate fully in this institution— or in many others—and that there is more afoot in the world of theological education than our eyes can see. Finding the future is not just about looking back to the past; it is also about looking at the present moment of diaspora and understanding how that affects how we do theological education in the global village.

To make sense of this past, present, and future, I begin by sharing my own hybrid narrative of how I became involved in theological education. Then I introduce the chapters of this book. My audience is those interested in theological education in a pluralistic context, especially those who work in institutions that already have large and diverse student bodies or anticipate increasing numbers of students from various diasporas. This book is also for those in an institution that is planning to launch a program aimed at one racial or ethnic group, especially the Chinese. My audience includes theological educators, trustees, and board members, those who invest in theological education through financial means or prayers, as well as administrators and strategists who are rethinking and reimagining the future of theological education in North America. Last but not least, my audience includes missiologists and mission-minded theological educators who are invested in what God is doing among diasporas around the world to fulfill the Great Commission of making disciples of all nations.

What do I mean by my own *hybrid narrative?* Japanese-Filipino-Canadian scholar Julius-Kei Kato defines hybridity as "people with many 'worlds' within them. These 'worlds' were once thought of as separate and distinct from each other, but they have now met, mixed, fused, and become part of the hybrid person's inner self."[1] That description resonates with my experience. Geographically and culturally, I have lived in three countries: China, Hong Kong, and the United States. My identity is a mixture of all three places, but none of them alone describes fully who I am and where I belong. I was born in Beijing, China, of Chinese-Vietnamese parents. That my parents were not born in China meant that I always knew and felt that I was different from the other students at my school. When my parents got together with their relatives, they spoke both Mandarin and Vietnamese. They also spoke Cantonese and some French, as was the norm for ethnic Chinese born in postcolonial Vietnam.

When I was ten years old, my family emigrated to Hong Kong, which was then a British colony. That experience transported me to a larger world, a world that required me to adjust to an entirely different culture, one marked by British colonial influences. For instance, the governor of Hong Kong was a white person who spoke British English, and the British national anthem was played every night on TV. There was no morning group exercise time as there had been in China. There was also no afternoon

3

nap. Instead, the island paused for afternoon tea. Living in Hong Kong meant I had to learn both Cantonese and English in order to fit in. While my parents struggled to survive economically, I struggled to acculturate. I was not always successful, especially in the first few years, for I was perceived as "a mainlander," inferior to the local Hong Kong girls, and hence often cast as an outsider. That was my first experience of being a migrant, a person betwixt and between multiple worlds.

My next experience of migration came when I left Hong Kong after finishing high school to go to college in Los Angeles, in the land of supposed freedom and endless possibilities. I came as an international student who had no intention of staying in the United States after graduation. But during my freshman year I came to know Jesus and then received a call to ministry. To pursue that call, I had to enroll in a seminary, and seminaries are more prevalent in the United States. And so my journey of theological education began. I had received all my higher education in the West, and that meant that I was immersed in Western ways of education—especially in theology, which I had not yet studied formally. It also meant learning from professors who were predominantly white and male. In my eleven years of seminary education, I had only one female Asian American professor and only one African American professor. As a result of the intersections of race, ethnicity, and culture in my life, I felt like a "perpetual foreigner" in a larger world, a person with a hybrid identity.

Because of the many "worlds" within me, to this day I wrestle with the question of how this kind of identity—a diasporic identity—fits with the mainstream theological landscapes in North America. Is there an educational model that embraces different "worlds" among students who are like me? I know I am not alone in this journey of searching for meaning while living in an other-dominated culture. Many Chinese were born outside of China, in Europe, South America, or Australia, for example, and speak French, German, Italian, or Spanish alongside Mandarin. There are also Korean-Russian, Chinese-Chilean, and Cantonese-Spanish dwelling among us and engaging in theological education. The ethnic identifier "Chinese" actually embraces a wide range of diversity and hybridity in itself. Such hybridity invites questions. Does language unite or divide different worlds? Is there room for other ways of thinking and doing theological education, ways that could honor both particularity and universality in a student body and in the larger ecclesial communities? I invite you to join me in wrestling with these questions in this book.

Upon earning a PhD in theology, I started teaching at Logos Evangelical Seminary in Los Angeles. Interestingly, my social location as someone with three cultures (Chinese, Hong Kongese, and American) almost parallels the three cultures (Chinese, Taiwanese, and American) of this institution, where I have been now for more than a decade. Although I share similar values with the Taiwanese Chinese, such as the proclivity for community and tradition, I have also inherited the Western ethos of individuality and openness. The hybridity of my growing up years is only compounded by the fact that I received my college and postgraduate education in the United States. But even here, I feel like a person who stands betwixt and between. This hybrid identity has become the norm for me. Culturally, I do not identify fully with Vietnam, China, Hong Kong, the United States, or Taiwan, for I am a mixture of all of the above. I am a "product" of the Chinese diaspora. When I worship at a local Chinese American church where three different congregations speak three different languages, the space where I feel most at home is one where people from the different congregations mingle in and across their different languages. It is from this intricate, hybridized, and diasporic vantage point that I write about theological education and the diasporic experiences that will shape the "next future" of theological education.

Traditionally, "diaspora" means "scattered" and "sowing." The term juxtaposes "home" and "abroad." Diaspora is a phenomenon that involves massive displacement of people from one country to another. However, for a person who lives and embraces multiple worlds, the ideas of "home" and "abroad" are fluid and ambivalent, as is that of "diaspora." For this book, the word has at least three different meanings. First, it describes my social location as one in which many worlds come together. Second, it describes the social location of the institution I serve. Third, it describes the present "in between" time in theological education. In a highly globalized and hybridized world, theological education in North America is at an intersection of between-times—a time between an established approach to theological education (what Ted Smith has called "Model M")[2] and a variety of emerging approaches; between face-to-face classroom teaching and virtual, online teaching; between a predominantly white student body and one that is increasingly diverse racially, ethnically, and culturally. Theological education now is between the times of past and present, between present and future, between now and when Christ returns. And as I hope you will discover in this book, this in-between time includes the persistent witness of the Chinese diaspora to the work of God among the nations. This diasporic state is a place where innovative ideas are generated, creative possibilities happen, and interconnectedness occurs.

This book is about theological education at a time in which miracles, church planting, diasporic displacement and migration, and fulfilling of the Great Commission are all happening at once. I write with a particular focus on the story of a group of Taiwanese Christians led by one person, Felix Liu, who started a movement—the Evangelical Formosan Church movement (the EFC). This movement ignited a fire that transformed Taiwanese Christianity in the West, extended its influence to the East, and continues to spread that influence among the Chinese diaspora and beyond. The unleashing of this force is changing theological education both in the East and in the West. This book is also about what God is doing among the Chinese diaspora in the context of theological education. Awareness of this divine activity will, I think, prompt the production of new resources and ideas for how we can educate Christians of diverse ethnic and cultural backgrounds in the future.

Chapter 1 tells of what God did through the life of one man in the Chinese diaspora—Felix Liu, the founder of Logos Evangelical Seminary—and how he responded to the Great Commission by yielding to the work of the Holy Spirit. Through him, God birthed a religious movement of church planting and evangelism that continues to expand around the globe.

Chapter 2 places the story of Logos as a counternarrative to the stories that have tended to dominate conversations about theological education. It also identifies challenges that a school like Logos has encountered and continues to encounter.

From the vantage point of this one seminary, chapter 3 features theological reflections on diversity through the lenses of language, ethnicity, and unity in the kingdom of God. It describes the Pentecost vision of the plurality of languages in theological education as a way of expressing the rich diversity of the kingdom of God.

Chapter 4 proposes a new narrative about theological education based on the previous three chapters. This chapter imagines what Logos Seminary would say to the wider communities of theological schools in North America and suggests how to continue such a dialogue.

The book concludes with a summary of the preceding chapters. As we will see, theological education between the times includes stories of multiple diasporic communities who desire to fulfill the Great Commission to make disciples of all nations. The story of Logos Evangelical Seminary does not fit into any narrative of decline. Rather, it tells of a new wave of God's continuing work among the nations, a new declaration of God's glory among all peoples (Ps. 96:3). I invite you to join me in this journey of discovering what God is doing through the Chinese diaspora to fulfill that ultimate purpose.

1

Yielding to the Spirit in the Chinese Diaspora

How does one individual shape an institutional direction and ethos? What are the meaning and *telos* of theological education from the vantage point of the Chinese diaspora? What does it mean to serve the global church and to participate in the Great Commission? What is the relationship between church planting, denomination, and seminary, and how do they function to advance theological education? This chapter tells the story of a man, a founder of a seminary, who has inspired others to reach for more, much more—indeed, to reach even for the kingdom of God. His life and legacy shape a theological school. His passion for the gospel enlivens his students. His ministry is changing the world from the periphery. And his influence will endure well beyond his times. This is the story of a man who yields to the Spirit, who bears witness to the work of God in the Chinese diaspora. It is also a story with important ramifications for the current state of theological education, and it might, I propose, illumine some alternative ways in which churches and seminaries together can meet the challenge of changing demographics.

Felix Liu is a Taiwanese immigrant who came to the United States, shaped a denomination that planted over a hundred churches around the globe, and founded a seminary to equip followers of Jesus to reach the ends of the earth. This seminary became the first ATS-accredited Chinese seminary in the United

States and spawned two other seminaries, one in Chicago and another in Taiwan. Here I recount the story of Liu, the influencer of a religious movement—the Evangelical Formosan Church (EFC)—that continues to change the landscape of theological education in the United States, among the Chinese diaspora and beyond.

The story of the Evangelical Formosan Church movement is the story of God's work through an individual—Felix Liu. Today, there are over 140 EFC churches around the globe. The first EFC church was started in 1970 in Los Angeles, and Liu became its senior pastor in 1975. In 1989 he became the first president of Logos Evangelical Seminary, a position he held until 2014. There is widespread agreement that Liu has been the driving force of the EFC throughout its fifty-year history. He is its symbol, authority, and inspiration. To know the EFC movement is to know Felix Liu. The bulk of his story that follows comes from my three interviews with him, and from a series of interviews with his co-workers and friends.[1]

Liu's childhood experience influenced and shaped his passion for healing ministry and evangelism. Liu was born with poor health and suffered from pneumonia, and consequently his mother often took him to see doctors. One of his earliest memories of his mother is of her holding him as a small and sick child and saying to him what would become her signature response in times of physical sickness: "Let us pray." Liu often suffered from lung problems and was unable to participate in sports as a healthy child would. Medication and prayer became two central elements of his experience of growing up.

Liu remembers another moment in which illness became a defining experience for him. When he was a child, his mother was bitten by an infected mosquito, which made her very sick. Eventually, the sickness became life threatening and was diagnosed as malaria. Malaria is often caused by mosquitoes that carry plasmodium parasites. The parasites travel to the liver to mature and then attack the bloodstream and cause blood cells to burst open. As the parasites infect more and more blood cells, the patient suffers from fever, headache, diarrhea, vomiting, and muscle pain. That Liu beamed with amazement while recounting this story to me indicated that the story might take a surprising turn. He said that while his mother was infected with malaria, she saw a vision of heaven in a dream. Heaven was so beautiful and glorious that she did not want to leave. We can only imagine that she must have seen something like what the book of Revelation describes—a city whose walls were made of precious metals; whose foundation stones were adorned with precious stones like sapphires, emeralds, beryl, and topaz; whose gates were resplendent with pearls; and whose streets were made of gold so pure it was transparent, like glass (Rev. 21:16–21). She must have dreamed of the river of the water of life, the divine throne, and the tree of life (Rev. 22:1–2). Liu said that she wanted to stay there forever and not return to Earth.

There and then, she dreamed of Jesus approaching her and saying in a gentle and kind voice, "Please return to Earth because your time has not yet come." Yet so struck was she by the awe-inspiring beauty of the heavenly scene and the comfort of divine presence, that she begged Jesus to let her stay in heaven. In her dream, she cried loudly and desperately. She begged Jesus, "No, I don't want to leave. I want to stay here. Please let me stay, please." She pleaded and pleaded so loudly that all of a sudden she awoke. She then realized it had been a dream. To her amazement, her malaria had left her. She was no longer sick. She had been healed instantly at the very moment that she awoke.

Whether the vision of heaven in her dream was real or not, we do not know. But it was real to her. Most importantly, her healing was real. Liu told me that this was his first encounter with instant healing. The incident planted a seed in his young heart and mind of what God can do in the here and now to an ordinary person. Her testimony left an indelible mark on Liu's life and paved the way for his later ministry of healing.

Liu's passion for evangelism began with his own experience of conversion. Liu was born to a Taiwanese pastor and his wife, the second son of six siblings. His grandfather was a pastor who dedicated his elder son, Liu's father, to God to become a pastor. Later, Liu's father in turn dedicated his elder son to God to become a pastor as well. Still today, the Liu family intends to carry on this sacred tradition. Since Liu's older brother was the "chosen one," Liu, as the second child, intended to support his brother financially. He thought of becoming a pastor himself, but he also realized that would require a clear calling from God.

Although Liu was raised in a Christian home, he did not experience the powerful presence of God until his senior year in college. Because a teaching assistant in one of his classes granted him credit he did not deserve, Liu felt tremendous guilt that haunted him for days. In reading the Scriptures sometime later, a verse struck him. That verse was Hebrews 12:1: "Therefore, since we have so great a cloud of witnesses surrounding us, let us also lay aside every encumbrance and the sin which so easily entangles us, and let us run with endurance the race that is set before us."[2]

Through this verse, Liu experienced God's forgiveness. Through it, he encountered a God who promised to guide him from that point on until he finished his race on Earth. As Liu contemplated his future profession, specifically whether to become a civil engineer or a pastor, another verse of Scripture spoke to him, 2 Peter 1:10: "Therefore, brethren, be all the more diligent to make certain about His calling and choosing you; for as long as you practice these things, you will never stumble."

Upon reading this passage, Liu asked God, "Are you calling me to become a pastor?" He felt that the answer was yes. Recalling that moment, Liu said, "This verse has carried me through my ups and downs from then to now. Whenever I face obstacles or troubles, this is the Scripture I go back to." Liu had received a call to ministry—the adventure of a lifetime of Christian ministry. This conversion experience was only one experience of many that demonstrate Liu's desire to yield his life to the Spirit.

After receiving the call to become a pastor, Liu enrolled at Tainan Theological Seminary in southern Taiwan. Upon graduation in 1967, he served as a chaplain at Chung Yuan Christian

University in Chung Li, Taiwan, working with and ministering to college students there until 1968. Between 1968 and 1970, he earned a master's degree in structural engineering at Chung Yuan and began teaching as a faculty member there, assuming that "the most effective way to reach out to the students is to become their professor." Almost four decades later, in 2006, Liu received Chung Yuan's distinguished alumni award for his contributions to and impact on the broader Chinese Christian communities.

From 1970 until 1974, Liu served as the chaplain of Tung Hai University in Tai Chung, where he developed his passion for personal evangelism among the student body. Many students, including the current president of Logos Evangelical Seminary, Dr. Kuo Liang Lin, became Christians during Liu's tenure at Tung Hai.

In 1974, Liu moved to the United States and enrolled in the master of theology in missiology program at the School of World Missions at Fuller Theological Seminary, with the goal of returning to Taiwan upon graduation to serve there.[3] Shortly thereafter, staff from the EFC approached him and asked him to lead the Evangelical Formosan Church of Los Angeles (EFCLA). Recalling that incident, Liu said, "I prayed for a long time whether to accept the invitation to pastor that church. I was planning on returning to Taiwan after finishing up my degree, but then the passage about Paul's Macedonian Call came to mind. I was thinking: 'Since I am studying Missiology and church growth, it is important that I practice it.' That was the reason I accepted the invitation. First, I thought they wanted me to serve as a youth leader. Little did I know that they wanted me to serve as the senior pastor!" Yielding to the Spirit took a different turn than Liu had first anticipated it would.

The Birth of the Evangelical Formosan Church

The church Liu went to serve—the Evangelical Formosan Church of Los Angeles—was the first Evangelical Formosan Church.[4]

Its story begins in the fall of 1965 in the Los Angeles area when several Taiwanese Christian immigrants joined Pastor George Chua's home church. In their house, the Chuas often cooked native Chinese and Taiwanese food, and this attracted many fellow Taiwanese. The Chuas, together with some Cantonese-speaking Christians, soon formed a Christian fellowship group and in May 1966 registered it under California law as the First Evangelical Church. In 1967, they bought a church building for Sunday services. In October of the same year, after Pastor Chua's departure for the Philippines, Rev. Eddie Lo assumed the position as pastor. At that time, English was the chief worship language, but on alternate weeks the service was also translated into Taiwanese and Mandarin to accommodate the parents of the church's Taiwanese Christians who were then starting to join their children in Southern California. Yet, as they were accustomed to speaking Taiwanese at home, it was awkward for them to worship in English and Mandarin on Sunday mornings. Therefore, beginning in the summer of 1970, the idea of planting a Taiwanese-speaking church emerged among six deacons of that church. These deacons believed there should be no linguistic barriers to worshiping God. Their proposal was soon accepted by the board of directors, the deacons, and Pastor Eddie Lo.

Although there was already a Presbyterian Taiwanese church in Southern California, they decided to go "independent" and plant their own church. On October 11, 1970, about forty Taiwanese-speaking Christians therefore left First Evangelical Church to form a Taiwanese-speaking church called Evangelical Formosan Church (EFC). The choice of the name "evangelical" was based on their belief that the church had to be gospel-centered. And the decision to include "Formosan" in the name reflects a particularly complex history. In the long history of internal conflicts that afflicted mainland China beginning in 1948, more than two million refugees from mainland China landed in Taiwan.[5] The island of Taiwan had been governed by several countries in its history, including Portugal, the Netherlands, and Japan. In 1517 the Portuguese named the island Ilha

Formosa, which means "Beautiful Island." The name Formosa as a designation for Taiwan endures to this day. Therefore, the term "EFC" distinguishes the church as Taiwanese as opposed to Chinese. For those who have lived in Taiwan for centuries, the term "Chinese" refers to those people who escaped from mainland China during Chiang Kai Shek's Nationalist regime in the 1940s and moved to Taiwan. In describing itself as "Formosan" rather than "Chinese," the church identified with the longer-term history of the island. But identities remain complex. Many Taiwanese speak Mandarin but still regard Taiwanese as their "heart language."

Instead of asking their supporters in Taiwan to assist the church financially, the founding members of the EFC in Los Angeles worked hard to ensure the financial security of the church themselves. They also allocated one-tenth of the church's monthly offerings for the missions fund and one-quarter for the church building fund. This church-planting effort was the birth not only of the Evangelical Formosan Church but also an Evangelical Formosan movement, a movement that continues to this day.

The congregation called Felix Liu to be their senior pastor in 1975. Liu started the cell group program, training church members to do personal evangelism and encouraging them to read Scripture on a daily basis. The church soon grew tremendously both in attendees and members, and by the end of 1977 had to relocate to a larger, newly bought church building in Highland Park that could hold four hundred people. However, Liu's vision for the church was not limited to that. He envisioned a church of at least one thousand members. To that end, Liu started to grow the church through church planting, and this became the way Liu participated in the Great Commission to make disciples of all nations.

In 1979, the EFC commissioned ten families to plant a church named EFC East Valley in the eastern part of the Los Angeles Basin. In 1980, a second church was planted in the southern district, in the city of Torrance, which later became EFC South

Bay. In 1982, another church planted in the northwest district grew to become EFC San Fernando Valley. In the same year, the movement planted EFC Orange County and then five more EFC congregations. This rapidly growing church-planting movement soon resulted in the launching of the EFC denomination.

The Founding of the EFC Denomination

What is the role of denominations in theological education? As more and more seminary students in the West have become responsible for their own seminary fees, the status and purpose of denominations have become ambiguous. However, the EFC, in addition to its help in financing church planting, provides scholarships to seminary students who serve at EFC churches. In 1982, the five newly planted EFC churches decided to stay united so as to encourage and support one another—not least in their efforts to support students—and consequently held a joint thanksgiving worship service to celebrate the formation of the EFC General Assembly (EFCGA), which marked the EFC as a denomination. The EFCGA wrote a constitution for the national body and revised bylaws for local congregations. Organizers also formed a board of directors, an executive board, and a ministers' association. A denomination was born. What is striking about the EFC denomination is that it was founded not in Taiwan but on US soil. Its headquarters remain here. As such, it is part of the religious history of North America. Christianity in the United States is not just about the dominant white and black races but also includes the Taiwanese and Chinese diasporic communities.

In addition to reaching out to Taiwanese immigrants, the five EFC churches developed English ministries geared to second-generation American-born Taiwanese. These churches also extended their ministries toward other Taiwanese-speaking churches outside of Southern California. For example, in 1984, a dying Taiwanese church in Saint Paul, Minnesota, joined the denomination and was revived through the help of EFC ministers. In 1985, a Bible study group in Denver and a Taiwanese church group in San Antonio also joined the denomination, and the EFCLA commissioned members who lived in the Arcadia area of California to form EFC Arcadia. The denomination supported a gospel fellowship group in Houston, which later became EFC Houston. That brought the number of EFC churches planted in the United States to ten.

Liu was a driving force in all these efforts. In 1986, while attending a Chinese mission conference initiated by the Chinese Coordination Centre of World Evangelism (CCCOWE),[6] Liu received a new vision encouraging him to "attempt great things for God; rescue millions of souls." The phrase comes from a saying attributed to English Baptist missionary William Carey: "Expect great things from God; attempt great things for God."[7] One day Liu read a newspaper report that hundreds of young people in Taiwan were engaging in car-racing events that often ended in death. Many of the younger generation in Taiwan were feeling lost and without a sense of purpose in life. Though many had the material means to sustain their lives, mentally and spiritually they often felt empty. Racing cars became a way to express their frustrations and hopes. Unfortunately, these events resulted in more death than hope. The fatality rate was so high that it was featured in the local newspapers almost every day. As Liu read about this, he perceived a deeper spiritual dimension behind the event. He pictured millions of young people racing to their eternal deaths by living without purpose. It grieved Liu that at that time Christians in Taiwan constituted only 2.7 percent of the population. The majority of the people in Taiwan had not even heard the gospel. Fearing that the rest would be lost forever, Liu vowed to rescue millions of souls.

Inspired by this vision, he made "Attempt great things for God; rescue millions of souls" the mission statement of the EFCLA and began working toward this vision right away. Shortly after the conference, Liu and his church coworkers spread out a map of the United States and identified ten places for their church-planting endeavor. Yet Liu's larger missional goal for the EFC was to plant twenty churches throughout the world by 1990. An astute coworker interrupted and noted, "The ten places we picked are the places we think we can plant the church successfully. If that is the case, where does faith come in?" In response to that inquiry, Liu said, "Okay, let's plant twenty-five churches by 1990 then." They named the vision "9025" to signal their commitment that by 1990 they would have planted twenty-five churches. When Liu recalled that moment some years later, he was still amazed: "How could ten churches become twenty-five churches in four short years?! But then, I learned that when we have the vision and the determination to do it, God will do his work. EFC churches began to multiply as a result." It was through 9025 that Liu truly launched his faith journey. It was yet another key moment that demonstrates Liu's practice of yielding to the Spirit.

In 1989, Liu and his team planted the twenty-second EFC church, this one in Costa Rica. Then Liu took a mission trip to Melbourne and Sydney in Australia and to Auckland in New Zealand. During that trip, about thirty people accepted Christ through Liu's ministry. These areas had many Taiwanese immigrants who were very receptive to the gospel. After that fruitful trip, the twenty-third EFC church was planted in Melbourne in 1989; the twenty-fourth church was subsequently planted in Auckland; and the twenty-fifth in Sydney in 1990. All these churches helped realize the 9025 vision ahead of schedule. By the end of 1989 there were eleven EFC churches in the greater Los Angeles area, fifteen churches elsewhere in the United States, one in Costa Rica, two in Australia, and one in New Zealand. Within about two decades of its inception, the EFC had planted thirty churches in four different countries, all because of the work of the Holy Spirit and one man's yielding to the Spirit. The EFC story is the story of God working through one individual, Felix Liu, whose chief purpose in life became to attempt great things for God and to rescue millions of souls for Christ. The gospel was propagated in the Chinese diaspora through Liu and his coworkers' efforts.

When asked, "What do you think of your accomplishment?" Liu would always respond humbly: "It was the work of the Holy

Spirit." He would continue by recalling, "When a person had a vision, others who are in the same Spirit shared the vision, and together they realized the vision with the guidance of the Holy Spirit." He would cite Acts 4:29-30 as the basis for his theological position on the role of the Holy Spirit in ministry. He would remind his interlocutor that after Peter and John were released from prison, they continued to do ministry and prayed to Jesus: "And now, Lord, take note of their threats, and grant that Your bond-servants may speak Your word with all confidence, while You extend Your hand to heal, and signs and wonders take place through the name of Your holy servant Jesus."

And Liu would comment, "The word of God and the work of the Holy Spirt collaborated to accomplish God's work." While Peter and John spoke God's word, they also practiced healing and signs and wonders. The word of God and the actual practice of ministry go hand in hand. In developing this line of thought, he also cited Genesis 1:2-3, "The earth was formless and void, and darkness was over the surface of the deep, and the Spirit of God was moving over the surface of the waters. Then God said, 'Let there be light'; and there was light." In Liu's view, Genesis 1:2-3 reveals the collaboration between the word of God and the Spirit of God in his creation. When God created light, he used his word "let there be light," but the Spirit of God also acted. It hovered over the surface of the waters. By mentioning both Scripture passages, Liu expressed his conviction that the word of God and the Spirit of God are inseparable to accomplish what God intends to do in the world.

Liu told me that miracles happened as he allowed himself to be the instrument of the Holy Spirit. These miracles manifested particularly in the physical healing of believers. Sometimes they occurred through prayer; at other times they came through particular circumstances and medications. He also mentioned that in his adult life, he had experienced physical healing. His own relatives, including his elder daughter and his brother-in-law, have also experienced physical healing. Through all these experiences of physical healings, Liu felt he had witnessed the work of the Holy Spirit firsthand and was compelled and called to participate in healing ministry.

The Shaping of Liu's Theology of Ministry

At the center of Felix Liu's teaching lie spiritual formation and its related discipline, holistic healing. Since the seminary's inception, his signature courses at Logos have been on these two related topics. For Liu, holistic healing requires spiritual, emotional, and physical restoration. As suggested by the title of his PhD dissertation ("The Relationship between Forgiveness and Christian Wholistic Healing in Biblical Study and Pastoral Ministry"), for Liu, spiritual formation is always rooted in forgiveness and healing in the fullest sense. The dissertation received the Theology Award from the School of World Mission of Fuller Theological Seminary in May 2000.[8]

For Liu, the purpose of forgiveness is healing. Healing results from the restoration of the relationship between humans and God—the "shalom" status. In Liu's theology of healing and restoration, one passes through four stages: (1) One has a harmonious relationship with God, people, and oneself. This is the ideal condition. (2) One encounters sin, sickness, and trouble in life. This is the imperfect condition of humanity. In this condition, (3) one needs to cry out to God and let him be the Lord in all areas of one's life, particularly those areas that are still under the domain of sin. (4) In this process of crying out to God, the person needs to deal with "inner garbage," that is, sin and emotional troubles, but the person can confess them and receive divine forgiveness. The relationship between forgiveness and healing, then, reveals God's motive for forgiveness, that is, to restore an alienated human being to fellowship and communion with him—the returning to the ideal "shalom" status (58–60).

Since the Lordship of Jesus Christ rights the wrongs in one's life, Liu asserts that one must remove anything that is unpleasing to him. A person should pray for the Holy Spirit to reveal to him or her any sins and then repent, so that God's healing and forgiveness can flow freely. In addition, Liu reminds us that forgiveness is not just a matter between an individual and God, but that it needs to be extended to other people. It is only by both receiving God's forgiveness and forgiving others that one receives complete healing, or what Liu calls "holistic healing" (70).

Further impetus for Liu's involvement in this ministry came in 1984 when Liu enrolled in John Wimber's course on "signs and wonders" at Fuller Theological Seminary. It shaped his philosophy of ministry, particularly in the area of healing ministry. Liu also attended Wimber's Vineyard church in Anaheim, where he witnessed many incidents of people instantly being healed. Vineyard church services had three primary components: worship, the message, and ministry. It was during the ministry period that miracles of healing often happened. Liu quickly recognized that Wimber was partnering with the Holy Spirit in ministering to those who came forward to receive the miracles of healing. He set out to do the same.

Liu developed a methodology for Christian holistic healing, which includes basic prayers for spiritual restoration and prayers for special needs. He indicated that "the primary purpose of the basic prayers for spiritual restoration is to restore harmonious relationship with God, with oneself, and with other people." The process he named "Basic Prayers for Spiritual Restoration" follows an orderly pattern and comprises five points (140–46).

First, one must welcome the Holy Spirit. Liu explains, quoting from Scripture:

> "The Spirit helps us in our weakness. We do not know what we ought to pray for, but the Spirit himself intercedes for us with groans that words cannot express. And he who searches our hearts knows the mind of the Spirit, because the Spirit intercedes for the saints in accordance with God's will" (Rom. 8:26–27). God has sent the Holy Spirit (John 14:16–26) to help us to discern God's will and God's way so that we can follow his will and his

way to pray for people. We all know that without the Holy Spirit's work, no one can confess that Jesus is Lord (cf. 1 Cor. 12:3). If not for the Spirit's work, no one could know God nor God's work. So, the first step in prayer for holistic healing is to welcome and open ourselves to the Holy Spirit.

Second, one must confirm God's word. Confirming God's word is what the author of the book of Hebrews refers to when he writes that "For the word of God is living and active and sharper than any two-edged sword, and piercing as far as the division of soul and spirit, of both joints and marrow, and able to judge the thoughts and intentions of the heart. And there is no creature hidden from His sight, but all things are open and laid bare to the eyes of Him with whom we have to do" (Heb. 4:12–13). When people trust in the word of God, his work will be manifest in their lives.

Third, one must accept the love of the Father and the Son. Liu states that "God's love is the foundation for the entire process of holistic healing prayer." Before one enters into healing prayer and asks God to come and touch one's life, one needs to know who God is. God is love. Since God sent his Son Jesus Christ to die for human beings as a way to show his love, what we need to do is open our hearts to accept this *agapē* love. Love makes us able to stand up and face all the problems we have. It also gives us the power to heal.

Fourth, one must accept Jesus Christ as the only Savior and Lord of our lives. Liu says: We need to commit ourselves totally without any reservation to him so that God's love by his Spirit can move freely within us. We not only need to receive him as our Savior who saves us from our sins, we also need to dedicate ourselves totally to him. We must let him be not only our Savior but also the Lord of our daily life, which means that we are willing to let him reign in every part of our life. After God's love comes into our hearts, we should willingly allow him to be the Lord of our lives.

Fifth, one must release anger and disappointment to God. For Liu, the barriers that arise between God and believers are sin. Therefore, one must confess one's sin and repent from it so that divine forgiveness can be granted and barriers can fall. Forgiveness involves the relationship between humans and God, humans and other humans, and each individual human being and his or her own self.

Throughout his teaching, preaching, and pastoral ministry, Liu practiced these five steps of prayer with his followers and witnessed hundreds of thousands of changed lives, including healings. At the core of Liu's conviction is the need for believers to cultivate a vibrant and intimate relationship with God. To Liu, nothing is more vital. Liu often tells students that studying theology or Hebrew and Greek is good, but it is nothing without an intimate relationship with God. He demonstrates this conviction through his daily practice of spiritual disciplines of prayer and meditation on the word of God. Liu acknowledges that "In the Taiwanese/Chinese culture, sometimes it is not easy for people to talk [or pray] about their problems" (165), so he identifies three levels at which a person can practice prayers: (1) One prays privately at a private place to reflect on one's inner condition. (2) If, after private prayer, a person still sees unresolved issues, then the person seeks an experienced prayer helper. (3) The experienced helper guides the individual in prayer (166). Liu cites James 5:14–16 as the scriptural support for this three-tiered prayer ritual.

That Liu himself practices such a vital prayer life is clear from an interview with Jonathan Siah, who has known him for over fifty years, first as a college friend, then as a coworker in Christian college work, then as Liu's student at Logos Seminary. Siah said, "Wherever Pastor Liu is, there is a ball of fire. Although Liu's temperament, appearance, and presence do not portray the image of fire, he embodies fire. That's who he is." Siah summarized his impression of Liu by noting three aspects of his personality: (1) he has an intimate relationship with God; (2) he has the gifts of healing, prayer, and evangelism; and (3) he has faith and conviction. What distinguishes Liu from others, said Siah, is that he is "one," meaning that Liu's life, his theology, and his spiritual gifts are all aligned and integrated. This is a mark of his spiritual formation. Liu's course on spiritual formation deeply affected Siah, and Siah has since taught spiritual formation at his church and in other ministry settings worldwide. Logos Seminary board member Scott Changchien echoes Siah's sentiments about Liu: Liu is "not the type of flamboyant-charismatic-prosperous gospel preacher. I think [he is] a 'Presbyterian on Fire.'" Another colleague of Liu, Ekron Chen, said: "What amazed me about him is the 'cleanness' of his spirit. He has either witnessed or personally gone through many disastrous crises in his career. He is definitely not naïve about the dark side of ministry and the sinfulness of human nature. Yet, the darkness does not seem to have touched him. Somehow, he maintains an innocence—a childlike faith in God." Perhaps it is also this childlike faith that sometimes frustrates those who work with him. For example, some say Liu cares much more about spiritual discernment than about intellectual analysis in decision making.

Of the many other testimonies about Liu's integrated spirituality, that of the current president of Logos Seminary, Kuo Liang Lin, stands out. Lin was a student in Tung Hai University in Taiwan while Liu was its chaplain, and Liu led him to the Christian faith. As a former student and then a colleague, Lin writes that "When Rev. Liu was the president of Logos seminary, although he was busy in many administrative duties, he was committed to teaching three courses: Personal Evangelism, Spiritual Formation, and Holistic Healing. I discovered that these three courses are intimately connected with one another. Liu's life and ministry also reflect these three inter-related areas."[9] Siah, Changchien, Chen, and Lin have witnessed Liu at first hand for decades, and their comments are all consistent about him. In a way, Liu is like the "Taiwanese Billy Graham" who desires and sets out to save as many souls as he possibly can. He speaks boldly and passionately against human sin and darkness and claims Jesus as the Lord of all. However, while Graham conducted evangelistic meetings, preaching the gospel to large crowds, Liu reaches out to the un-reached through healing meetings. Liu has also ministered to countless individuals personally to bring them to God. While Graham was typically visible on a culturally prominent stage, Liu is more typically to be found ministering "quietly" among the Chinese in the Chinese diaspora, hidden from the English-speaking world yet active in the sight of God.

Liu's primary target audiences are the Taiwanese and Chinese in North America and in the Taiwanese and Chinese diaspora. While he has been successful in conducting healing ministries worldwide, he admits that "sometimes, after prayer, people still have not received healing. Forgiveness issues are sometimes present; sometimes issues of God's sovereign will and Christian suffering and trials are involved; psychological and psychiatric issues and the bondage inherited through generations sometimes exist. There are many other issues that need to be studied regarding healing" (227). While some may cast doubt on Liu's way of interpreting Scripture, that does not change the fact that Liu has made a tremendous contribution to the ministry of restoration through fervent prayers and the holistic healing process.

During Liu's ministry, the work of the Holy Spirit has been manifested not only in individual healing but also in church growth. In less than five decades, the original EFC movement has evolved from one church in Southern California to a denomination in its own right that is expanding on a global scale. By the year 2000, 51 EFC churches had been planted, and by 2010, there were 84 worldwide.[10] The vision for the denomination is to plant 200 EFC churches around the globe by 2020. Liu and his ministry colleagues named this vision "the EFC 2020 Jubilee." In 2020, the denomination intends to celebrate its fiftieth anniversary in Taiwan. Many EFC church delegates from around the world will gather in Taiwan to celebrate this historical moment and to witness fifty years of God's work among the Chinese diaspora and beyond. In Scripture, "Jubilee" refers to a fifty-year cycle, at the end of which all land is returned to the original owner, with no need for compensation because the land belongs to the Lord

(Lev. 25:10–17). In this light, Elder Jay Kuo, former moderator of the EFCGA, said, "The year of Jubilee starts with the sounding of loud trumpets on the Day of Atonement (Lev. 25:9). When EFC celebrates the Jubilee in the year 2020, we hope that it will be a big day of reconciliation with God and that God's people will return to him."[11] That the present book's publication in 2020 coincides with the celebration of the EFC jubilee I prefer to see as God's providence and not mere coincidence.

Liu mentioned to me in an interview that for a movement to last, the key person has to be there for a considerable length of time. He reckons that if he had left after his first, second, or even third term as the senior pastor of EFCLA, the EFC movement would not have persisted and thrived in the way it has. That is a profound insight for ministry and leadership. The EFC story is indeed a story of how the Holy Spirit worked among the Taiwanese and Chinese Christians in the Chinese diaspora.

Liu's ministry has always had two key trajectories: healing ministry and personal evangelism. Both trajectories are rooted in spiritual formation, for to Liu one's spiritual condition informs and determines other aspects of one's life. For him, one's personal relationship with God is the most significant aspect of one's life as a Christian, something that transcends one's particular knowledge, gifts, and service. So when some people suggest on the basis of his healing ministry that Liu is too involved in the charismatic movement, he responds that his ministry is simply based on the word of God as well as the Holy Spirit. He cites the story of Jesus healing a blind man as an example: "And they came to Bethsaida. And they brought a blind man to Jesus and implored Him to touch him. Taking the blind man by the hand, He brought him out of the village; and after spitting on his eyes and laying His hands on him, He asked him, 'Do you see anything?' And he looked up and said, 'I see men, for I see them like trees, walking around.' Then again He laid His hands on his eyes; and he looked intently and was restored, and began to see everything clearly" (Mark 8:22–25).

Liu sees himself as following Jesus's example. He considers himself a vehicle, one who points people who need healing to the Holy Spirit. He refuses to be placed in the same category as those who perform signs and wonders, instead considering himself simply as partnering with the Holy Spirit. Judging by the outcome of his healing ministry, Liu has the gift of healing. Yet when I asked him, "Do you think you have the gift of healing?" he responded, "No, I don't. I just pray."

Indeed, prayer defines Felix Liu. Whenever the name Felix Liu is mentioned, students imagine him folding his hands in prayer, or getting down on his knees to pray. Appropriately enough, there is a sculpture of hands in prayer in the prayer garden on the campus of Logos Seminary. They are none other than the praying hands of Felix Liu.

That said, one's strength is also one's weakness. Liu is a human being with his own limitations. Because Liu tends to see everything through a spiritual perspective, some people think he oversimplifies things. Others would say he is not a skilled administrator, although he is a great fund-raiser. His wife, from time to time, has lamented that Liu is always outside doing ministry, implying that she wishes he would spend more time at home. Yet God has blessed Liu with a family of four daughters and over a dozen grandchildren. To this day, all his children and children's spouses are active in ministry—in itself a testament to his spiritual strength and legacy.

The story of Felix Liu shows how God uses ordinary persons in the grand mission of salvation to reach those previously unreached through church planting, personal evangelism, and healing ministry. It also shows how the life of one individual can shape the course of a seminary and its curriculum—and how it can shape the world far beyond that one place. As part of his teaching ministry, Liu has traveled extensively, and consequently his fame and influence have spread across Taiwan, Australia, New Zealand, Brazil, and North America, particularly among the Chinese and Taiwanese diaspora. The EFC movement has been shaped by Liu and will continue moving forward. Liu not only is a contemporary saint, he is also a visionary, a charismatic leader, an evangelist, a wounded healer, a church planter, a teacher, an administrator, a spiritual authority, and a humble servant. His legacy will be remembered and carried on through the EFC movement as well as through his many students and family members who follow his path.

Theological institutions often start with an individual. And Logos started with Liu. Liu's life yielded to the Spirit has shaped a seminary that is also committed to yielding to the Spirit and to centering its theological ethos on spiritual formation. In the current Chinese diaspora, students from China and from all over the world come to Logos to receive theological education. However, that is changing. In recent years, many students have enrolled in the "fully" online master of arts program at Logos. But these students are still required to come to campus for the spiritual formation course. How to do spiritual formation online has been a constant challenge among theological schools. At the time of this writing, the spiritual formation course at Logos is therefore still taught face-to-face. This further demonstrates the centrality of spiritual formation in the educational culture of Logos Seminary. That centrality is only one of Liu's many legacies.

The Birth of Logos Evangelical Seminary

What is the purpose of theological education in the EFC context? What is the relationship between church planting and seminary education? As we have seen, EFC churches have grown rapidly not only in North America but also in other regions of the world. But that has brought with it a serious problem—the lack of professionally trained pastors to minister to these newly established congregations. Liu's experience of hiring pastors from Taiwan and transporting them from one culture to another did not seem to work. Although they spoke the same native language as the church people, the immigrant culture in North America is different from the culture back home. For example, the illustrations of the sermons did not fit the immigrant context, and the applications pastors suggested during their sermons often did not meet the needs of the immigrant church context.

In light of this, Samuel Kao, a coworker of Liu with a particular vision for theological education, suggested training local Taiwanese immigrants to minister to these Taiwanese-speaking churches. The idea encountered opposition at first. Some were concerned about the lack of resources to implement such a plan; others were more generally doubtful about the plan's success. Eventually, to assist the EFC denomination's missional and church planting tasks, the EFC General Assembly started a Taiwanese seminary to address the EFC shortage of pastors. The result was the founding in 1989 of Logos Evangelical Seminary. Liu served as its president for its first twenty-five years (1989 to 2014). The Chinese name of the seminary was originally Tai Fu Seminary, "Tai" being short for "Taiwan" and "Fu" meaning "Gospel or Evangelical." The name alone reminds us that the seminary did not arise in a vacuum but was a response to the needs of the Taiwanese-speaking churches. The planting of these churches was due to Liu's vision for the kingdom of God, namely, to rescue lost souls. Naturally, Liu became the first president of the seminary while also pastoring Evangelical Formosan Church of Los Angeles. This dual position lasted for several years before Liu assumed the presidency of the seminary full time. Not surprisingly, the motto for Logos is Liu's own adaptation of William Carey's: "Attempt great things for God; rescue millions of souls." A student recalled Liu's impact on him during his seminary days, remembering the time Liu preached a message focused on this motto. That motto has since shaped the student's perspective on how to become a faithful servant in ministry. After hearing the sermon, he asked Liu to pray for him and his family. He remembered that Liu held his hand and prayed for him fervently. That image of Liu has left an indelible mark on the student's mind and life that remains to this day.[12]

Logos Evangelical Seminary is distinctive in being the first seminary dedicated to the Chinese-speaking community that is accredited by both the ATS and the Western Association of Schools and Colleges (WASC). Several Chinese seminaries in North America have now pursued accreditation. For example, China Evangelical Seminary in North America in Los Angeles was founded in 1992 and was accredited by the ATS in 2015. Christian Witness Theological Seminary in San Jose, California, was founded in 1973 and received ATS accreditation in 2016. In this sense, Logos Seminary has been a leader in directing the future of Chinse theological schools in North America.

With its vision of planting churches in Taiwan, in 2007 Logos established a seminary in Taiwan—Taiwan Logos. Its mission is to equip and train ministers for the churches in Taiwan.[13] In 2009, because the greater Chicago area needed a Chinese seminary, Logos also started a branch campus there, meeting the needs of the Chinese churches in that area and the shortage of pastors in the Chinese churches in the Midwest. In other words, since its beginnings, the mission of Logos has been to attempt great things for God and for the global church. Though at first its primary target was Taiwanese-speaking churches, this mission later expanded to include Mandarin-speaking churches. Logos Evangelical Seminary now serves as a training ground for the global church, particularly for the Chinese diaspora. In this sense, planting churches and growing churches to worship the glorious and great God are the *telos* of the Evangelical Formosan Church movement. The founding of the seminary only serves as the means to that end. For the EFC, the meaning and purpose of theological education are always missional and global.

Felix Liu was not alone in establishing Logos Seminary. From the beginning, he had two strong teammates: Silas Chan and Wilfred Su, both of whom had received doctorates from Fuller Theological Seminary. Liu served as president of the seminary and focused on fund-raising. Chan focused on academic affairs, and it was his idea to seek ATS accreditation. He was also active in many ATS functions, and at the ATS bicentennial meetings in 2002, he was invited to give a benediction from his wheelchair at the end of the worship service. He was the first Chinese academic dean to have the honor of doing so. Chan has been Liu's ministry partner for almost two decades. He passed away in 2014, just a few months before Liu himself stepped down from his presidency.

Su was in charge of the administrative and financial aspects of the school. He also maintained strong personal relationships with students, alumni, and pastors that continued even after he retired. Even now, he frequently travels around the world recruiting students and strengthening graduates' bonds with the seminary. I recently asked him how he got involved with Logos Seminary. He recounted an incident with Liu. Su had a habit of going for a stroll after dinner. One day Liu joined him on his walk, and began accompanying Su regularly on his daily walks. At first they chatted casually, but one evening Liu invited Su to join Logos Evangelical Seminary as a coworker, and Su accepted the invitation. After that, Liu stopped walking with him. As Su recounted this event with me, we both smiled. Su retired from full-time teaching at Logos in 2015 but continues in adjunct teaching and ministry around the world. Together, Liu, Chan, and Su formed a trio that built Logos on solid ground.

In 2014, after serving as president of Logos for twenty-five years, Felix Liu stepped down. Since then, he has spent considerable time in Taiwan with his wife, ministering to people there and teaching a spiritual formation course at the Logos Taiwan campus. He also conducts healing ministry events all over Taiwan, the United States, and other centers of the Chinese diaspora such as Rome, Sydney, and Auckland. Although Taiwan is Liu's homeland, his base is still in Los Angeles, where his family, children, and grandchildren reside. Whenever he is in Southern California, he likewise preaches, teaches, and conducts healing events at various churches. He continues to be incredibly effective, still living out his motto.

At a recent Logos school retreat, a new female student brought her unbelieving husband along. As a faculty member, I wanted to be friendly, and so I approached him and welcomed him. On the final day of the retreat, the female student brought her husband to me again, but this time to tell me that he had just become a Christian—because Felix Liu had shared the gospel with him the day before. This was typical: while my goal at the retreat had been to be friendly and welcoming toward all the guests and especially new students, characteristically Felix Liu had the gospel in mind and, as ever, reached out to those who had yet to know Jesus. Now as then, Liu preaches the word, whether in season or out of season (2 Tim. 4:2).

Learning from Liu's Story

The focus of this chapter has been the life, ministry, and legacy of Felix Liu and how God uses such a person to shape a denomination and a theological institution. Liu is behind the Evangelical Formosan Church movement that started in the greater Los Angeles area and gradually spread to other parts of North America, Asia, and beyond. From one person grew a denomination, over a hundred church plants, and an accredited seminary. So what? What are the larger implications of his ministry? What does his ministry mean for yours? I turn our attention to four specific consequences.

The Work of the Holy Spirit in the Diaspora

The story of Felix Liu is a believer's story, an EFC story, an immigrant story, and most important of all, a story of God's mission among the Chinese diaspora. Migration and immigration continue to change the demographic, racial, cultural, political, and economic landscapes of the United States. While these landscapes keep evolving with each new wave of immigrants, the religious consequences of such changes are sometimes overlooked. Writing from a Hispanic American perspective, Daniel Carroll, in his monograph *Christians at the Border*, recounts the complicated issue of Hispanic presence in America, and how it challenges "who we are" as a nation, its impact on jobs and services, and how the general public has a predominantly negative view of undocumented immigrants.[14] He discusses the challenge of the Hispanic presence in America and points out that their Christian faith is a largely ignored dimension of their presence here. "Most Hispanics arrive in the United States with some type of Christian background and awareness," he writes. "Christian faith is vibrant among [the] immigrant population, which now numbers in the millions."[15] Millions more have come to faith after their arrival in the United States. Together, these populations have contributed to the "browning" of Christianity in this country.[16] Carroll remarks that it is very likely that God has brought millions of Hispanic Christians to the United States to revitalize the Christian churches here. As a result, the church of Jesus Christ is growing and being affected by the faith of these immigrants in unexpected ways.[17]

In a similar vein, the Taiwanese Christian presence in America exemplified by Felix Liu and the EFC movement has ignited a fire that not only kindles the faith of fellow Taiwanese Christians in the United States but has also affected the Taiwanese diaspora and subsequently the Chinese diaspora around the globe. This fire is like an unstoppable force that will keep going strong to "the ends of the world" because it is ignited by the Holy Spirit. The vision that Liu and the whole EFC denomination received fifty years ago testifies to the fact that God poured his spirit on them and enabled them to see visions and dream dreams for the kingdom of God. The collaborative effort of human initiative and the Holy Spirit continues to transform Taiwanese and Chinese Christianity in the Chinese diaspora.

The change that Liu has brought and that his work continues to bring started at the periphery, on the margins of Taiwanese immigrants in the United States. This margin has widened with time and expanded to Taiwan itself and other regions around the globe. The increasing numbers of second-generation Taiwanese and Chinese Americans who speak neither Taiwanese nor Mandarin have pushed first-generation Taiwanese and Chinese Christians to look beyond themselves. Hence, many EFC churches in North America, New Zealand, and Australia have begun to form three congregations under the same roof or on the same church campus: the Taiwanese-, the Mandarin-, and the English-speaking, to meet the different linguistic and cultural needs of their members.

The expansion of EFC churches in the Chinese diaspora reflects not only the current state of Christianity in the world but also the current landscape of religion in America. Just as Hispanic Christianity is renewing churches in the United States, so too the growth of the EFC churches contributes to Christianity in the United States and around the globe. Both Hispanic and Chinese diasporic Christian communities impact not only a single ethnic or racial group but also the whole world. They demonstrate that God's kingdom includes people from all nations. The growth in EFC churches demands appropriate theological education to form those who will serve these churches. Logos Evangelical Seminary exists for the global church. Its mission is always being renewed and reshaped to meet the changing landscape of theological education in response to global and local needs. At the beginning of the thirtieth anniversary celebration of Logos Seminary in September 2019, its mission statement was once again renewed, this time to "Forming missional servants for God's kingdom; Transforming global churches for Christ." This renewed mission statement reinforces the ethos of the seminary to engage in global missions for the global church.

A Cord of Three Strands: Seminary, Church, and Denomination

From the story and journey of Felix Liu's ministry, we see a close relationship between seminary, church, and denomination and how these three components interact and strengthen one another. While theological education in the West has shown a general weakening of denominations and of voluntary societies (as Ted Smith's book in this series mentions), the EFC offers a powerful counterexample. While students in the West are increasingly on their own financially without support from a denomination, the EFC shows strong denominational financial support for students. And while many seminaries and denominations are experiencing strained or weakening bonds, Logos Evangelical Seminary and the EFC denomination remain tightly linked. They share a mission of serving the global church, particularly in the Taiwanese and Chinese diaspora. There are strong reciprocal relationships between the EFC churches, the EFC denomination, and Logos Seminary. The EFC churches follow the vision of the EFC General Assembly but also contribute financially. Each EFC church donates a certain percentage of its annual offering to the denomination to support the denomination's global church-planting effort. In addition, the denomination governs the structure and provides organizational leadership to the churches, and the churches follow the bylaws established by the denomination. The founding of the seminary by the denomination serves the vision of the denomination to plant churches and to spread the gospel to the ends of the earth.

In discussing the importance of the theological school–church relationship, Dan Aleshire remarks that "a meaningful relationship with ecclesial bodies is crucial for theological schools."[18] He quotes Michael A. Battle, former president of the Interdenominational Theological Center, that "the church is necessary for the seminary, but the seminary is not necessary for the church."[19] The statement is true in its emphasis on the importance of the church for the seminary. Without the church, where would seminary graduates go? What purpose could the school serve? But EFC and Logos show a deeper mutuality and reciprocity than Battle suggests. For if seminaries fail to train competent pastors, how will the church grow? True, the church could establish its own theological schools in the form of an organized Sunday school or hire professional theologians as speakers and teachers to conduct systematic theological training for congregations, but even these people would have to be trained somewhere. Given the closeness of this relationship, the seminary's curriculum design needs to be relevant to the needs of the church. Aleshire says the future "depend[s] on both the church and the school seeing the relationship they share as important and vital."[20]

Currently, the EFC provides scholarships for students who serve at EFC churches. However, many students from Logos Seminary do not attend EFC churches or serve the denomination upon graduation. As the seminary moves beyond the denomination to embrace other denominations and churches, its original purpose to train ministers for EFC churches has been shifting to preparing ministers for the global church. But even when placements go beyond the institutions of the EFC, the mission of the school remains closely in tune with the EFC. Given this harmony of mission, it seems reasonable to expect that the relationship among Logos Seminary, EFC congregations, and the EFC denomination will remain close. This intricate web of relationships creates "a cord of three strands" that is not easily broken.

The Meaning and Purpose of Theological Education

The theological education that Felix Liu received and later practiced in his own cultural context provides a glimpse of the meaning and purpose of theological education. Shaped by the teachings of Peter Wagner and Charles Kraft and the example of John Wimber's ministry, Liu practiced in his own ministry what he learned from his mentors. In his journey, we see the significance of theological education and how it informed and transformed his ministry. The theological education Liu received at Fuller Theological Seminary defined the theoretical and theological basis for his future ministry. In his life and ministry, theology and practice are two different but interrelated areas. Theology shapes practice, which in turn refines theology. They reinforce one another. When he teaches spiritual formation, Liu often reminds his students to journal the insights they receive from Scripture in their daily devotions. He encourages them to locate one verse or one phrase from Scripture that speaks to their hearts. Over time, this daily practice of reading Scripture will develop into a habitual practice that will continue to form the basis of their ministries of preaching, teaching, and caring for others. For instance, when he read "the Lord will accomplish what concerns me" in Psalm 138:8, he took it to heart and used it to pray that God's purpose would be fulfilled in other people's lives.

The theology of Liu's healing ministry is grounded in his theological understanding of the healing power of God in the Old Testament as well as the healing ministry of the earthly Jesus as recorded in the New Testament. While Liu studied the theology of healing in his theological education, his own healing ministry was informed by observing how others practice that ministry and applying that to Taiwanese and Chinese cultures. Here again, we see that the practice of theology has to be contextual to be effective.

For Liu, theological education went beyond mere knowledge to integrating that knowledge into real life and ministry practices. The meaning of theological education, then, is first and foremost to transform the lives of students by encouraging them to develop a healthy and vibrant relationship with God as well as build a solid foundation of biblical principles, and then applying that knowledge in one's ministry context. For Liu, the *telos* of theological education is to change lives to conform to the purposes of the divine Creator and Lord of all. This is compatible with the EFC vision to fulfill the Great Commission in making disciples of all nations. Changing lives is a way of making disciples. The story of Felix Liu helps us to reflect on the meaning and purpose of theological education, not only in North America but also in the rest of the world. As Lois McKinney Douglas writes, "globalized theological education is rooted in *missio Dei*, celebrates spiritual formation, affirms the missional nature of the church, and emerges from hermeneutical communities."[21] Liu's integration of theory and practice in his life and ministry demonstrates this *missio Dei*. His teaching on spiritual formation provides the theological groundwork for his healing ministry as well as the passion for personal evangelism. The church-planting effort of the EFC movement continues to participate in the grand mission of God. His "hermeneutical community" is located in the Chinese and Taiwanese diaspora. Felix Liu has contributed not only to the landscape of Chinese and Taiwanese Christianity for the future but to Christianity and the broader religious landscape in America.

The Future: Rethinking Language and Majority

If the story of Felix Liu and his impact on the Taiwanese and Chinese communities had not been told in English, it would have been unknown to the Western world, and Western understandings of theological education in the twenty-first century would be missing a significant piece. While it is one thing to converse on the subject of theological education within one's own theological tradition, such as within the Reformed, Pentecostal, or Roman Catholic heritages, it is another and even more narrow thing to converse on one's theological practices in one's own native language without disseminating those ideas to a wider audience. In writing the story of Felix Liu, I cannot help but recognize the necessity of communicating the stories of significant influencers or spiritual giants in a language that the majority can understand. I am certain there are stories of other remarkable individuals in other countries that are told only in their native languages and have not yet been translated into English. In this in-between time, the English language has functioned as a shared if contested space that connects people of different languages. In this sense, language divides but also unites. One of the consequences of the tower of Babel event in Genesis 11 is the separation of people groups because of differences in language. But the Pentecost event in Acts reversed what happened at Babel, and people from different dialects and tongues were enabled to understand each other without interpreters. I will address more fully the issue of language and ethnicity in relation to theological education in chapter 3.

Knowing the story of Felix Liu also presses us to rethink the definition of "majority." What is the language that the majority of twenty-first-century people speak? It is not English. Over 1.2 billion people in the world speak Mandarin; 400 million speak Spanish; English comes in third with about 360 million speakers.[22] According to these statistics, the Chinese would be in the majority, having the largest population in the world, but as I write the story of Felix Liu, I am compelled to write it in English, the perceived "majority" language. Isn't there an irony here? In missional terms, the "majority world" refers to so-called third world countries in Asia, Africa, and Latin America, whereas the "minority world" is identified as North America and Europe. If we intend to write to a wider audience, we should be writing to the majority world. Though at this moment in the twenty-first century English is still the international language where people with different first languages can connect, how long will this continue? In a hundred or a few hundred years, is it possible that Mandarin or Spanish will replace English as the premier international language? The now "majority world" might one day truly become the majority world. If and when that time comes, the present margin would become the new center. As the Hispanic and Chinese diasporas renew Christianity globally, the flipping of margin and center in the future will be the natural consequence. Yet, the ultimate renewal of Christianity awaits not just this reversal but also the new heaven and new earth where all nations will come together and sing God's glory in one accord.

This chapter is about how God uses a person to propagate the gospel, and how that person's story shapes a denomination and a theological school to contribute to theological education in the Chinese diaspora and beyond. This chapter is also about the work of the Holy Spirit in the Chinese diaspora in the twenty-first century, and thus it illuminates the present and future landscape of theological education. This leads us to the next chapter, in which I tell the particular story of Logos Evangelical Seminary, a seminary in the United States that uses Mandarin as its instructional language. As I indicated above, perhaps this way of speaking and of being a seminary will become a part of the "next future" of theological education. I will reflect on this seminary's way of doing theological education as a distinct trajectory in its own right, but also as a trajectory that runs counter to dominant narratives in theological education in North America. It is worth a second look.

Countering Dominant Narratives in the Diaspora

As the series title, Theological Education between the Times, suggests, theological education is at an in-between time in which old waves of theological education are receding and new waves are emerging. Ted Smith's book in this series identifies signs of the times that include declining enrollment and ongoing financial difficulties that have led several prominent theological schools (including Andover-Newton, Episcopal Divinity School, Seabury Western, and Bangor Theological Seminary) to close, merge, or embed themselves within larger institutions in order to continue to fulfill their missions. Recently, Fuller Theological Seminary announced a financially driven move from its historical location in Pasadena to another Los Angeles suburb, Pomona, and then changed its mind and will stay in Pasadena but with significant downsizing. In 2019, two Southern California seminaries were contemplating relocating in order to address financial concerns: Claremont School of Theology will be relocated to Oregon, and International School of Theology has moved from El Monte to a church facility in West Covina.

Yet not all schools are telling this story. Logos Evangelical Seminary is a thriving seminary serving a global community of Chinese Christians to minister in the Chinese diaspora and beyond. While several schools are relocating or downsizing to address financial issues, Logos is renovating its campus. What is more, all the funding for renovation has been provided by faithful supporters of the seminary. Although financial crises have been a part of the Logos story from time to time, by God's grace the school has come through every crisis. There is, after all, something new emerging in the enterprise of theological education in the twenty-first century, although with struggles of its own.

This chapter focuses on Logos Evangelical Seminary as part of that emerging wave of theological education and as a countervoice that speaks to the contemporary currents of theological education in North America. The story of Logos provides an alternative vision for theological education, one that helps us to reflect on the meaning and purpose of theological education between the times. After identifying several ways in which Logos offers up that counternarrative, I reflect on the contributions and challenges of a seminary like Logos and close with some reflections on the future of theological education.

Logos Evangelical Seminary as a Counternarrative

As a diasporic seminary in the United States and the first Asian seminary accredited by the Association of Theological Schools (ATS), Logos Seminary both conforms to the educational standards of the association and diverges from its typical forms. I would highlight in particular seven divergences:[1] (1) Logos is helping to pioneer theological education that stresses *formation*; (2) Logos focuses more on forming servants than on forming leaders; (3) Logos pioneers by using Mandarin as its instructional language; (4) Logos regards the MDiv degree as the path to pastoral ministry; (5) Logos strongly supports the role of women in ministry; (6) Logos's students incur minimal educational debt; and (7) Logos has launched a PhD program for future theological education in the Chinese diaspora. Each of these divergences counters the general trajectories of dominant narratives among theological schools and allows Logos's voice to be heard clearly in the roar of old and new waves of theological education.

Logos Is Helping to Pioneer Theological Education That Stresses Formation

Across ATS schools, more and more seminaries emphasize spiritual formation or a formational model of education. Daniel Aleshire's book in this series discusses these developments in greater detail. Using broad strokes, Aleshire paints the development of this model and projects it as the "next future" of theological education. While formation may be the "next future" for many schools, at Logos Seminary the primacy of spiritual formation has been emphasized since the founding of the school. In chapter 1, I introduced the founder and first president of Logos Seminary, Felix Liu. Due to his philosophy of ministry, which centers on spiritual formation, he, and by extension the seminary, gives priority to students' intimacy with God over their knowledge of Scripture, history, systematic theology, and skills for ministry. He believes being precedes doing; that is, one's relationship to God precedes ministry. His course on spiritual formation not only functions as his "signature course" but also has become the signature course of the seminary as a whole. Logos graduates take pride in having taken this course. Many graduates have shared publicly how this course has shaped or transformed their lives and their philosophy of ministry and identify spiritual formation as their foremost educational experience.[2] Many entering students also mention that the school's emphasis on spiritual formation is the reason they chose Logos. Indeed, for Logos, spiritual formation has been at the heart of its mission since its founding.

Throughout the history of theological education in the West, two fundamental educational models have coexisted and at times collided. David Kelsey calls them "Athens" and "Berlin." The focus of the Athens model is on shaping the soul through character formation and holiness. Its goal is to know the good in the sense of acquiring moral and intellectual virtues. It tends to focus on the students, helping them to experience formation by cultivating their own personal appropriation of wisdom about God and themselves in relation to God. The Berlin model, on the other hand, has dual foci—*Wissenschaft* and professional education. *Wissenschaft* refers to orderly, disciplined critical research, whereas the goal of professional education is to train ministry professionals. The goal of *Wissenschaft* is to teach students how to engage in research and master the scientific and objective truth of the subject they are studying. The Berlin model helps the students to move from data to theory to application of theory to practice.[3] We may distinguish these two modes of educational models as the "formation model" and the "research-professional model."

Beginning in the last third of the nineteenth century, the Berlin model rose to dominate higher education in the United States.[4] However, in recent decades more and more theological schools have been paying close attention to the importance of formation in theological education. For them, how their students are formed and shaped into the program's desired learning outcomes has become more important than the previous focus on the research-professional model. One of the main skepticisms regarding online education has to do precisely with the difficulty it has integrating the formation aspect of learning into the online format, since formation seems to work best through face-to-face interactions. While in previous decades the West (and most theological schools in it) has prioritized the research model over the formation model, at Logos Seminary the formation model has driven the educational philosophy of the seminary since its inception.

In her book *Cultural Foundations of Learning: East and West*, Jin Li researched the different learning styles of European American students and East Asian students. She found that the former tend to view the goal of education as learning to master the world whereas the latter perceive it as a process of transforming the self. While the learning style of European American students is mind oriented, the learning style for East Asian students is virtue oriented. The mind-oriented learning style privileges active engagement, critical inquiry, and self-expression, whereas the virtue-oriented learning style centers on earnestness, diligence, concentration, and developing the capacity to endure hardships.[5] In other words, the educational model of East Asia as a whole is focused on character formation, much like the model Kelsey associates with Athens. The virtue-oriented learning style is based partially on the teachings and influences of Confucius, who, though he was not a Christian, did believe in the idea of "heaven" and the existence of a supreme being.

In the West, besides the poles of the Berlin and Athens models, there exist the mystic traditions and teachings of people such as Julian of Norwich, John of the Cross, Bernard of Clairvaux, Gregory the Great, and Teresa of Ávila. For these thinkers, spirituality and the communion between God and human souls take primacy in the formation of believers. We should add Thomas Merton, who called twentieth-century Christians to contemplation; Henri Nouwen, the Catholic priest whose writings on spirituality have exerted great influence in recent decades; as well as more contemporary figures like Richard Rohr and David Benner. While Logos prides itself on emphasizing the significance of spiritual formation, it is not alone. Yet, in the historical development of educational models among *evangelical Protestant schools*, Logos's spiritual formation program runs against the grain of most mainstream theological schools.

In *Beyond Profession: The Next Future of Theological Education*, Dan Aleshire reflects on his own experiences of theological education. He discovered "an educational outcome that was less about knowledge gained (or forgotten) than perspectives or sensitivities that have formed me and endured with considerable stability."[6] He predicts that many things will change in the function and practice of theological schools in the future of theological education, but that the spiritual and human qualities that authentic religious leadership requires will remain one of its significant needs. He cites 1 Timothy 3:1–7 and Titus 1:7–9 regarding the ethical and religious qualities of clergy, and argues that these two texts call for renewed attention and cultivation. These spiritual qualities of religious leadership, I believe, are precisely what Logos transfers from the past into the present and future. The primary difference between Felix Liu's formational model and Aleshire's lies in the scope of formation. For Liu, formation is rooted in one's relationship with God, which then flows out of one's life and conduct. For Aleshire, the understanding of formation is broader in that it includes the whole educational goal in theological education and the educational process that the goal requires. Much of what Aleshire describes in his book reflects the educational ethos of Logos, namely, that the goal of theological education is holistic, involving intellectual, affective, and behavioral formation. While the formation model is the "future" of theological education in the West, it has been an underlying constant in the educational ethos of Logos Seminary from its beginning.

Logos Focuses More on Forming Servants Than on Forming Leaders

In the educational philosophy of the West, the recent shift from equipping students for vocational goals to forming leaders in God's kingdom has been made apparent through a renewed understanding of the purpose of theological education. Therefore, spiritual formation and character formation have become a vital part of curriculum design in many theological schools. The goal of theological education for these schools, then, is to form future leaders. For example, the mission statement of Fuller Seminary is: forming global leaders for kingdom vocations. The mission statement of Gateway Seminary is: shaping leaders who expand God's kingdom around the world. And the mission statement of Emory University's Candler School of Theology is: educating faithful and creative leaders for the church's ministries throughout the world. As we can see, these mission statements share similar words such as "forming," "shaping," and "educating." They also indicate the extent of their mission by the synonyms "global," "world," and "kingdom." And they stress the significance of forming "leaders," a term presumably intended to include not just pastors but also religious workers of many kinds. All these ministries are gathered under the title of "leader."

In the past, the mission statement of Logos Seminary was about equipping servant-leaders. In the ethos of the seminary, the signifier "leader" connotes the idea of leading, which may or may not be connected to service. A leader in the Chinese context may be someone who dominates over others or who is competent but also arrogant. The seminary always wanted to resist this model. In 2019, the president and the seminary's stakeholders took this commitment a step further by dropping the word "leaders" from "servant-leaders." The new mission statement begins with "Forming missional servants." This move further reinforces the goal of theological education at Logos as being to form servants, not necessarily leaders. The idea behind the change is that a servant is someone who exemplifies humility, gentleness, and willingness to serve others, someone who does not exert his or her will over others but helps, listens to, and blesses those he or she serves. This reflects the virtue model and creates a countervoice to the dominant narratives in the West. While the West may say having a strong voice is a strength in ministry, it is not so at Logos. For Logos, an attitude of humility and servanthood is more highly prized as a virtue. Logos stresses formation, as other schools do. But its formation has a distinctive aim: Logos seeks to form people as humble Christian servants. What the West prides as virtue may not be so at Logos.

Among immigrant churches in North America, it is rather common for churches to split. Strong personalities often cause chaos and dissension in church politics. I have talked to many Chinese pastors over the years about recruiting the right kind of seminary students to work at their churches. The common quality they desire is someone who can follow, not someone who can lead. They want people who can obey the leadership and follow the direction of the church rather than be innovative and assertive about their own agenda. Their past experiences of hiring strong personalities have often resulted in church splits.

Given this fact, forming servants rather than leaders may well be the right thing to do in the Chinese context of North America.

In the West, self-assertion of one's individuality is perceived as a positive character trait, whereas at Logos it is deemed a negative quality. Standing out from the crowd is not perceived as something to celebrate. Instead, what is highly valued is humbly serving others without drawing attention to oneself. The reality is that churches and ministries need both leaders and servants. We cannot have a whole bunch of servants without leaders to lead them, nor can we have a whole bunch of leaders without servants to work alongside them. Therefore, tension exists in theological schools between forming a servant and forming a leader. The outdated term "servant-leaders" may endure the test of time in the context of Chinese Christianity in general, and Logos Seminary in particular. Forming servants who will lead humbly and effectively will remain a continuing challenge in the future of Logos Seminary.

Logos Pioneers by Using Mandarin as Its Instructional Language

Logos is the first ATS-accredited seminary to use Mandarin as its primary instructional language. While the majority of ATS schools situated in North America instruct their students in English, Logos is doing a new thing. Logos Seminary's initial vision was to train ministers for the newly founded Evangelical Formosan Church (EFC) congregations in the United States, New Zealand, and Australia. Since the EFC denomination originated among Taiwanese Christians, planting Taiwanese churches and training Taiwanese ministers were natural responses to the denomination's church-planting intention. However, two major events shifted the mission of the school from the original one of being a Taiwanese seminary to being a Chinese seminary, therefore expanding the school's influence to a global scale.

The first event occurred in 1994 when James Hudson Taylor III—the great-grandson of James Hudson Taylor, a British missionary to China and founder of Overseas Missionary Fellowship (OMF, formerly the China Inland Mission)—came to visit Logos and proposed that the school engage in a so-called midcourse correction, specifically to change the language of instruction from Taiwanese to Mandarin. In light of the increasing number of Chinese immigrants in the United States as well as the seminary's intention to meet the needs of the Chinese churches around the globe, Felix Liu and his leadership team accepted Taylor's proposal. Mandarin is generally regarded as the official Chinese language, as opposed to Chinese dialects such as Taiwanese or Cantonese. That was the first step that Logos Seminary took to reach beyond people of Taiwanese descent to a broader set of Chinese Christian communities worldwide. This change enabled non-Taiwanese-speaking students and faculty to join the seminary.

Logos's second shift took place in 2007: the seminary changed its name. That the original Chinese name of the seminary had the word "Tai" (short for "Taiwan") in it conveyed an image of a seminary that existed for Taiwanese-speaking people only. Therefore, a strong conviction of Liu and his leadership team prompted an elaborate process of "name realignment"—aligning the Chinese name of the seminary to its English name, Logos. The name of the school changed from Tai-Fu Seminary to Zheng-Dao Seminary. "Zheng-Dao" reflects the meaning of the Greek word "Logos," that is, "the Word." This name change marked a milestone in the vision and history of the seminary. The new name, Zheng-Dao, not only aligns with the English name Logos but also attests to the fact that "Logos is a denominational seminary serving inter-denominational needs." While the school would not lose sight of ministering to the EFC's needs, its greater goal is to make disciples of all nations through equipping servants who work for the kingdom. This kingdom perspective has since attracted non-Taiwanese students to Logos. While the change of instructional language to Mandarin in 1994 opened the door for students from China, the large influx of students of Chinese background did not begin until after the seminary's name change in 2007.

Since the name realignment, the number of students with a Chinese background—students who either are citizens of China or claim a primary affiliation with China—has increased significantly, especially from 2014 to 2019, when such students jumped from 38 percent of total enrollment to 67 percent. In 2007, Logos established another campus in Taiwan, where students of Taiwanese background enrolled; this resulted in fewer students from Taiwan coming to Logos's main campus in California. Yet I believe the trend of students coming from China to North America will continue into the near future. However, the extent of immigration will shift along with factors such as politics, economics, and international relations.

More and more students from China with English as their second or third language choose Logos Seminary for theological education largely because its instructional language is Mandarin. In addition, students from elsewhere (including the United States) whose primary language is not English but Mandarin have found a place at Logos, where they can converse, learn, study, and write papers in their native tongue without any language barriers. Logos believes using one's primary language as the instructional language increases educational effectiveness and enhances students' learning experience.

In American culture, non-English languages such as Spanish, Russian, Mandarin, and Korean are often scorned. Persons who do not speak English well are generally considered "inferior" to or less intelligent than those who speak perfect English. In academia, this phenomenon of using English as a mark of intelligence largely persists. It is important for students to have the chance to learn without this stigma. In addition, since the majority of graduates of Logos intend to serve the Chinese diaspora upon graduation, learning the Scripture and practices of ministry in the Chinese language prepares them for their future ministry contexts. Based on these factors, it is important that there be a place in theological education for instruction in one's native tongue, be it Mandarin, Cantonese, Korean, or Spanish. I address the language issue more extensively in the next chapter.

While on the faculty at Logos, I have also had opportunity to teach at other seminaries in the United States and at schools in

Brazil, Spain, New Zealand, and multiple Asian countries. One of those US seminaries is Fuller Theological Seminary in Pasadena, California, where I have taught students whose primary language is not English and who possess limited English verbal skills. Some have only just arrived from other places such as South Korea or South America, while others have been living in the United States for a while but only in their ethnic community and thus have limited command of English. Students with limited English verbal proficiency mostly remain silent in class and are not able to engage in group discussions. Sometimes I wonder whether it would be better for those students to use their native tongue for their theological education. After all, upon graduation they will most likely serve their own ethnic churches, which use their own language. Wouldn't it be more effective to take up theological education in one's own native tongue?

For some minority or international students with limited English skills, another significant factor contributes to their choice of a mainline Protestant or English-speaking evangelical seminary over an ethnically centered school at which they might be able to use their native language: prestige. In the cultural mindset of many minority students, being able to enroll and graduate from a well-known English-speaking theological school is a sign of prestige, a reflection of much-desired upward mobility, a form of achieving "the American Dream." Likewise, many ethnic churches may perceive a diploma or degree from an English-speaking institution to be preferable to one from an ethnic school. Therefore, the idea of "prestige" has two aspects: the perception of the students as well as the perception of the "market value" of the degree. But these are not the only factors on students' minds. During admission interviews at Logos, I encounter students who choose to come to Logos not because of their limited English proficiency or the image of Logos as an ethnic seminary, but because of the missional factor: they know an education at Logos will prepare them well for their future ministry in the Chinese context. Therefore, one's future cultural context of ministry is also a factor in choosing which theological school one will attend.

Logos Regards the MDiv Degree as the Path to Pastoral Ministry

Most theological schools have long considered the MDiv to be a professional degree. Such schools consider it their primary goal to train ministers for the church. The MDiv degree is emblematic of that goal. This is especially so in the Chinese Christian context; most Chinese churches require this degree of their pastors. An MA degree in theological schools simply does not match up to the expectations of such churches. In the Chinese Christian culture, a person who earns an MDiv degree is perceived as a minister of the gospel and is considered to be on track to becoming an ordained pastor, assuming the person has no major flaws in character or morality. Such churches do not expect the same of someone with an MA degree in theology or a related discipline.

At Logos Seminary, all students who apply for the degree programs are required to interview with the admissions committee, which is composed of the academic dean, the dean of students, and select faculty members. Unmarried students attend the interview alone, but married students are expected to bring their spouse to the interview. If a student desires to transfer from an MA to an MDiv track, that student is likewise required to bring his or her spouse to the admission interview. If committee members sense any lack of support in the spouse of the MDiv applicant, they typically reject the applicant, under the assumption that when the student becomes a pastor, it will be helpful if not essential for the spouse to support the pastor's life and ministry. No other degree programs include the applicant's spouse in the interviewing process, and this fact sets it apart from other degree programs at Logos. In the West, the fitness for ministry relies mostly on the individual alone, whereas the participation of Logos leadership and faculty in the assessment of students' fitness for ministry aligns with its emphasis on spiritual formation. Being a pastor is not an individual matter but a family matter, a communal matter.

Another distinction of the MDiv degree at Logos is that, to pass the admission interview and gain approval of the committee, the applicant must be certain of his or her calling to become a pastor upon graduation. In fact, the purpose statement of Logos's MDiv program specifies that its objective is "to prepare students for effective pastoral ministries in various settings." If the committee senses any uncertainty in the applicant, it either approves the applicant for an MA degree or suggests study courses other than the MDiv for the applicant. In short, at Logos—and at Chinese seminaries in general—the MDiv degree is regarded exclusively as a professional degree reserved for future ministers and pastors. The involvement in assessing the students' fitness for ministry depends partially on the admission committee at Logos. The admission committee members function as "gatekeepers," ensuring as far as is possible applicants' callings to become ministers or pastors. There are cases in which academically qualified MDiv applicants are rejected because they lack a clear calling or commitment to future pastoral ministry. Interestingly, when these rejected students apply to English-language seminaries in Southern California, they are usually accepted. The difference in the understanding of the MDiv degree at Logos and in the Anglophone seminaries could not be more striking.

Statistically, based on the ATS Strategic Information Report for Logos Evangelical Seminary for the 2019 to 2020 period, the enrollment for all programs has grown steadily over the past ten years, though MDiv enrollment shows a slight decline in the past two years. The current enrollment of 170 students is above its average enrollment of 163 for the past decade.[7] Moreover, the placement rate of MDiv graduates at Logos has been above 80 percent since 2013. In 2017, it reached 100 percent, meaning that in 2017 all MDiv Logos graduates had found a paid ministry job by the time they graduated.[8] In 2019–2020, the MDiv placement rate is 85 percent. Although it has declined slightly, this percentage is still remarkable when compared to all other ATS schools in the same year, among which MDiv placement is 75 percent, with evangelical schools at 71 percent, mainline schools at 75 percent, and Roman Catholic schools at 81 percent.[9]

Moreover, in 2019, the MDiv graduation rate at Logos was 92

percent, which is the highest rate of all ATS schools, whose average is 62 percent, and more specifically, 51 percent at evangelical schools, 72 percent at mainline schools, and 72 percent at Roman Catholic schools. (See figure 2.1 below.)

Figure 2.1.
Graduation rates by degree and ecclesial family for 2019

	Logos Seminary	All ATS Schools	Evangelical Schools	Mainline Schools	RC/Orthodox Schools
M Div	92%	62%	51%	72%	72%
Professional MA	50%	52%	49%	67%	51%
Academic MA	37%	54%	48%	60%	57%
Advanced Professional	45%	48%	43%	55%	40%
ThM/STM	0%	54%	44%	66%	60%
ThD/PhD		48%	52%	44%	48%
Overall	52%				

What is more, at Logos those enrolled in the MDiv program have always attained a higher graduation rate than those seeking the MA degree. One reason for this is the clear purpose of the MDiv program—training future ministers and pastors. Another is that the program admits only students who are certain of their vocational calling to become a pastor and have their spouse's support. At Logos, the MDiv program equips future ministers. The school provides resources to achieve that end. The goal is for future ministers to transform individuals and society through pastoral ministry. The MA is more open ended. The culture at Logos assumes that all students, in one way or another, are future pastors, even though many students in the MA programs do not plan to enter pastoral ministry. But the MDiv's insistence on greater clarity and commitment on the front end seems to make for higher rates of graduation and higher rates for placement.

Logos's MDiv program looks a lot like what Ted Smith calls Model M, that is, a model in which "theological education provides resources for ordained work of leading a religious institution that works for the transformation of individual lives and wider society."[10] The irony is that Model M has been degenerating and diffusing in the wider world of theological education in the West as students, faculty, and curricula begin to pull away from this goal. For instance, theological schools may not be able to provide the required resources for students for ordained ministry. Students who come to theological schools may not aim to do paid work at a religious institution. Or they might want to be paid to work full time in ministry but also know that is very unlikely. Additionally, the goal of some religious institutions is not the transformation of individual lives and wider society but the advancement of research and publication (the Berlin model), which may contribute to the changing identity of the MDiv degree as well. At these institutions the pursuit of academic scholarship takes precedence over the traditional model of theological education that prepares students to be ministers. Perhaps a new model needs to emerge. I will address the status of the MDiv degree further in the final chapter.

However, while Model M is breaking down in many English-speaking schools, at Logos Model M still stands as of now. With that said, as I mentioned earlier, enrollment in the MDiv program at Logos has declined in the past two years. This could be attributed to the increase of other degree programs, such as the MA in Family Ministry and the MA in Intercultural Studies. The increased number of Chinese programs at other schools may also be a factor. This decline also demonstrates the changing nature of theological education between the times. Yet the conviction and perception of the MDiv degree at Logos and among Chinese seminaries as the path to pastoral ministry remain strong for now.

Logos Strongly Supports the Role of Women in Ministry

Many evangelical Protestant seminaries display deep ambivalence about the role of women in ministry. Some discourage women from engaging in any teaching or preaching ministry in which they have authority over adult males. Others oppose or prohibit women from being ordained as ministers of the gospel. Still others do not allow women to take on leadership roles at theological institutions. Even when the faculty supports women in ministry, the trustees and board members may find the idea offensive and contrary to their theological convictions. And even when a whole school supports women in ministry, the school may be part of a larger ecology of churches that does not. Women can graduate with credentials for ministry but fail to find suitable work as ministers.

Logos does not fit this narrative. It is proudly evangelical in its mission and identity. And it strongly supports women in ministry in a wide range of capacities, including serving as senior pastors of mixed-gender congregations, preaching from the pulpit, and taking on significant leadership roles in various religious organizations. For example, at least three alumnae have become presidents of Chinese seminaries, specifically, a Bible college in Myanmar, a Bible college in Hong Kong, and a seminary in Taiwan. Over one hundred female graduates are either actively engaged in preaching ministry or serve as ministers or ministry directors at different churches and organizations. Overall, at least eighty female graduates out of over seven hundred alumni serve either as the lead pastor or as associate pastor in Chinese churches worldwide. Figure 2.2 shows the placement of female MDiv graduates at Logos from 2000 to 2019.

Figure 2.2 reveals that 43 percent of female MDiv graduates from 2000 to 2019 are involved in congregational ministry, more than any other form of ministry, which indicates that the MDiv is, on one hand, still the standard route to pastoral ministry at Logos and, on the other hand, the chief avenue by which women can attain a position in pastoral ministry. In general, more male than female MDiv graduates are expected to go into pastoral ministry, but the high percentage of female MDiv Logos graduates participating in pastoral ministry is hard to ignore.

Additionally, the gender distribution of students at Logos between 2000 and 2019 has remained relatively steady, with male students averaging percentages in the fifties and female students in the forties. The MDiv degree still attracts more male students, mostly because it is the route to ordination, a role traditionally reserved for males. The MA in Christian Studies degree attracts higher numbers of female students, and the ThM degree, which has historically attracted roughly the same number of male and female students, in recent years has enrolled more females than males. The DMin program has consistently attracted more male than female students owing to the predominance of male pastors in Chinese churches. The newly launched MA in Family Ministry degree initially had all female students and still has more female students than male students.

As regards faculty, in the academic year 2019–2020, seven of Logos's fourteen faculty members were women. Logos retains a higher percentage of female faculty members than other evan-

Figure 2.2.

MDiv Women Graduates Ministry Placement 2000–2019
(N=86)

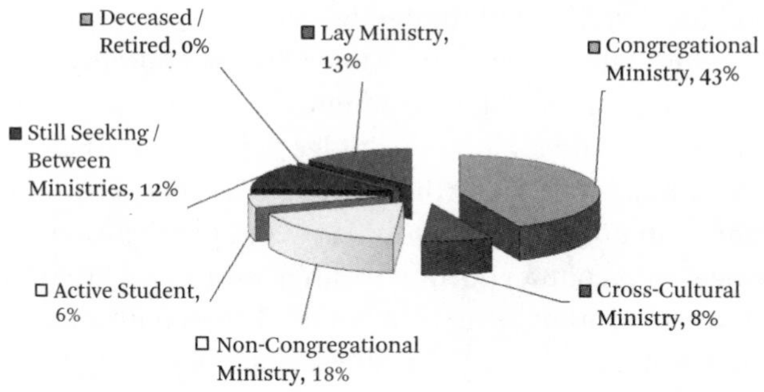

Source: Logos Evangelical Seminary

gelical Protestant schools in Southern California, and may boast the highest percentage of all. Fifty percent of faculty members at Logos are women. As such, it serves as a countervoice to the other evangelical Protestant schools among the ATS member schools, which average 16 percent female faculty.[11]

What is more remarkable is not just the number, but what the number represents. Four of the seven female faculty members at Logos teach either Bible or theology. Usually, schools that are ambivalent about women in leadership assign them to areas like counseling and Christian education, not Bible and theology. Thus, Logos offers yet another counternarrative to the stories usually told about evangelical schools. Not only that, but as of 2020, at Logos, one of the seven female faculty serves as the academic dean, one as the assistant dean, one as the director of family ministry, and one as the chair of a significant committee. Other female faculty members without leadership positions are all active preachers in local churches. There are other leadership positions available at Logos, and the leadership is ready to accept any qualified female faculty person willing to take on the responsibilities. At Logos, the issue is not whether there are leadership positions available for women or whether the leadership approves or disapproves of women taking those posts. The issue is whether female faculty members *want* those leadership positions.

While Logos Seminary supports women in ministry and women ordination in its fullest sense, the culture of majority Chinese churches, especially in the United States, shows a strong preference for male lead pastors. Most of these churches therefore prefer to hire a male MDiv graduate over a female one. This accounts for the relatively low percentage of Chinese female pastors in the United States. Nevertheless, Logos's support of women in ministry is an undeniable fact that is worth highlighting. This commitment runs counter not only to other evangelical Protestant schools but also to other Asian cultures marked by patriarchy. Korean churches, for example, like Chinese churches, struggle with the role of women in ministry. In the hierarchy of Korean culture, the male pastor is often perceived as a revered authority figure.

The role of women in ministry there is consequently extremely challenging. Of course, there are important exceptions. And many schools, both mainline and evangelical, support Korean and Korean American women in ministry. Some congregations welcome women's leadership. But it is still more the exception than the norm for a Korean woman to be allowed to speak from the pulpit. Though a thorough discussion of gender dynamics in the Korean culture is beyond the scope of this book, this reality further highlights the distinction of Logos Seminary in supporting women in leadership. Logos stands out in relation to both evangelical Protestant traditions and Asian Christian traditions in this regard.

Additionally, Logos's support of female leadership also runs counter to Chinese heritage. That heritage is shaped by the Confucian notion that women are inferior to men and have to obey men in all aspects of their lives, from birth to death.[12] As a Chinese seminary, Logos's respect for women invites curiosity.

Why does Logos support women in ministry? One reason is the EFC denomination's belief in the equality of men and women. Although Logos is not being particularly intentional in supporting women in leadership roles, its support for women in ministry does reflect the school's commitment to forming both men and women as missional servants for God's kingdom. It recognizes that the mission of God includes both genders and that supporting the equality between both genders is simply biblical.

Another reason is the lack of qualified bilingual males applying for the jobs. There is also a practical matter. Since the salary of most pastors at Chinese churches in the United States is higher than that of professors at Chinese seminaries, qualified male applicants frequently choose to pastor a church instead of teaching at a Chinese seminary. Also, Chinese churches have a strong preference for male pastors, which leaves female seminary graduates fewer available pastoral positions. Therefore, teaching and working at theological institutions seem like a more viable option for them. The story is complex. But the commitment is clear—and quite distinctive in relation to a number of the traditions that have helped shape Logos.

Logos's Students Incur Minimal Educational Debt

In these times between the times, financial strain has caused more and more theological schools either to shut down, relocate to a less expensive location, or cease conferring degrees. With the breakdown of Model M in most theological schools, this trend is likely to persist. On the students' side, educational debt incurred in seminary threatens the viability of their future ministry. It can often take students more than a decade to pay off their student loans. According to the ATS, in the academic year 2016–2017, about half of the students at ATS schools graduated with no educational debt while the other half incurred debt ranging from about $20,000 to about $40,000,[13] and a little more than half of those had debt ranging from $40,000 to $60,000.

By contrast, at Logos Seminary, in the same period, MDiv students incurred no debt whatsoever. About a third of students in the academic MA program did take on some debt, but the total averaged less than $10,000.[14]

The statistics in Jo Ann Deasy's study also show that the higher a student's age, the lower his or her debt. This can be explained by the generally greater financial stability of older students compared to their younger counterparts. Students in their twenties incurred the most educational debt, as did PhD graduates. This is owing to the higher cost of earning a PhD as well as the relatively longer time span involved in pursuing that degree.

If graduates are able to land a job upon graduation, that gradually eases their financial burden. However, the reality is not always encouraging.

Given the gloomy reality of educational debt across ATS member schools, Logos Seminary's track record offers yet another counternarrative to this general trend. At Logos, students have used all their means to minimize debt throughout their theological education. ATS conducted a survey, "Graduating Student Questionnaire, 2017–2018," with twenty-five respondents, to gather data on the educational debt incurred at Logos in the academic year 2017–2018. As of June 27, 2018, of the twenty-five participants in the survey, twenty-three had not incurred any educational debt, which is far better than the situation at most theological schools.

Various factors contribute to students' low educational debt. First, Logos has been recognized as one of the most affordable theological schools in the United States.[15] In admission interviews, many students indicate that affordable tuition is one of the reasons they choose Logos. How sustainable this financial situation is remains unknown, but based on the history of the school, financial sustainability is a goal and journey of faith in which the leadership and the whole Logos community participate. Second, Logos provides significant financial aid to students who need it. The funding for that comes mainly from faithful donors who desire to invest in theological education. Continuing to cultivate relationships with these donors and attracting new donors are an ongoing endeavor of school leadership. Third, because federal loan programs such as FAFSA (Free Application for Federal Student Aid) are not available to international students, who constitute more than half of Logos's student body, these students must be self-funded or receive financial support from their home churches or from the churches they serve. Therefore, these students incur less debt. Fourth, since students in the PhD program are most likely to incur educational debt owing to the length and cost of the program, Logos annually provides five full scholarships to admitted qualified PhD students. This scholarship is primarily credited to the fund-raising efforts of Felix Liu, who shared the school's strategic vision for training future theologians and theological educators for Asia with potential donors, who then offered overwhelming financial support for the program.

The school does have financial struggles, however. Almost every year, Logos fears not meeting its budget, and many times its operating costs are at risk. At every one of these moments, both the former president and the present president have led the school in fervent prayers. Amazingly, miracles do happen, and they happen over and over again. As an evangelical seminary, the financial piece becomes another way to practice spirituality, relying on God for the provision of one's need.

Some of these counternarratives can be traced more or less to the value of Chinese culture and tradition. As I mentioned earlier, the traditional Chinese culture centers on the virtue model (formational model). In this model, education is about the whole person. It involves not just the intellect of the person but also the person's heart, mind, and soul. Thus, the current mission statement, "forming missional servants," reflects this educational ethos. The use of Mandarin as the instructional language is owing to the demographic of Chinese immigrants and people from the Chinese diaspora. Chinese churches around the globe need Mandarin-speaking pastors and clergy, and naturally the existence of a Mandarin-speaking seminary responds to the need of the growing Chinese immigrant churches in the diaspora. The perception of the MDiv degree as the path to pastoral ministry has been ingrained in the Chinese Christian tradition. MA seminary graduates are accepted as pastors in some Chinese churches, but they are mostly hired as specialized pastors in youth ministry, children's ministry, or family ministry. Except for a few special cases, rarely does an MA graduate become the senior pastor of a Chinese church.

I do not wish to generalize or simplify what Chinese culture entails, but one thing I observe is that Chinese people, particularly first-generation immigrants, like to save rather than spend their earnings. They like to purchase property and prepare financially for their children. Many do not want to be in debt. It is a common practice that Chinese parents are responsible financially for the cost of college education for their children. When the children reach eighteen years old, they are not left alone and treated as adults. Instead, in many Chinese families, children always remain children—including financially. Students at Logos incur minimal debt not just because of a church's or the denomination's support but also because of Chinese culture itself. Every culture has its distinct values and drawbacks. Perhaps some of these Chinese values can serve as a helpful reference for the West in doing theological education as a communal effort rather than an individual matter.

Logos Has Launched the PhD Program for Future Theological Education in the Chinese Diaspora

While a higher research degree program like the doctor of philosophy has long been a part of the academic world in mainline seminaries and evangelical Protestant seminaries in North America, it is no small matter when a diasporic school like Logos has a PhD program that has been accredited by the ATS and the WASC (Western Association of Schools and Colleges) Senior College and University Commission (WSCUC) since 2014. As of spring 2020, Logos is the only theological school among Asian and diasporic schools in the United States that offers a PhD program in Bible. This forms yet another counternarrative to diasporic schools and Asian seminaries in the West. The cost of running the program, the demand for academic resources, as well as having qualified faculty to teach are all challenges facing this program. Yet the funding has been provided by faithful donors to the seminary. Logos's close proximity to Fuller makes it possible for Logos to use Fuller's library resources. Logos also hires esteemed adjunct faculty from other American seminaries to supplement the faculty pool. The launching of the PhD program at a diasporic school like Logos itself reflects a miraculous work of God.

While the PhD program at Logos follows the "Berlin" model in its academic rigor, the primary vision for launching it was not to shape future theological educators in the West but to provide theological education in Asia and the Chinese diaspora. Its incorporation of the contextual element in the curriculum design distinguishes it from other PhD programs in the West. Perhaps this distinction contributes to the accreditation of the program by the relevant agencies. The challenges of recruiting qualified students are still considerable, since students with strong English-language proficiency tend to enroll in Anglo seminaries. The program is still relatively new and awaiting further development, yet launching it successfully with the vision to serve broader theological education in the Chinese diaspora is worth mentioning, for the mission of the program—to provide a next generation of faculty for theological schools throughout Asia and the global Chinese diaspora—is distinctive.

Logos takes distinctive steps in other areas as well. For instance, while the center of the school's work is preparing people for ministry, Logos also provides education for laypeople through an extension program known as the Logos Training Institute (LTI). LTI trains laypeople in the greater Los Angeles area, and its online courses reach the Chinese diaspora beyond Los Angeles. About one-third of LTI students eventually enroll in degree programs at Logos. The LTI also offers supplemental nondegree programs such as "Kairos," a course on missions similar to "Perspectives," that encourages students to orient their lives toward the missions of God. The seminary exists for the church. Logos Seminary continues to shape the current state of theological education in North America and to make its mark in the future.

Contributions of Diasporic Seminaries

As more seminaries rooted in diasporic communities join the ATS, theological education will be challenged and enriched by the global networks these communities sustain. In this section, I identify three contributions of a diasporic seminary like Logos and in the next section three challenges such a seminary is encountering. I believe these findings will help the larger academic and ecclesial communities reflect on their own practices of theological education and at the same time catch a glimpse of what God is doing in theological education between the times.

Missiology

According to the final report of the Asian Schools Peer Group, "Educational Models and Practices in Theological Education," sponsored by ATS in 2017, "one conspicuous feature of the Asian

(Chinese and Korean) schools is that all are rooted in the post-1965 ethnic immigrant communities. There were 3.8 million Chinese Americans and 1.7 million Korean Americans during the 2010 census." Immigrant churches become the space not only for religious gathering but also for ethnic and cultural preservation and continuation. Owing to the influx of Chinese and Korean immigrants, Chinese and Korean seminaries play an important role in their ethnic communities and in their identity formation. The same report also identifies nine ATS member schools that are predominantly Asian; three other Asian schools maintain candidacy or hold associate status with the ATS. Nine of these twelve schools are located in or near Los Angeles County. With its population of 1.5 million Asian Americans, Los Angeles has become "the capital of Asian America." From Logos's faith perspective, Los Angeles has become the hub of the global mission field. Gateway Seminary (formerly Golden Gate Baptist Theological Seminary) has relocated from San Francisco to Los Angeles precisely because it realized Los Angeles is a burgeoning mission field.

Owing to the strong transnational connections between Asian immigrants in the United States and their home countries, immigrant churches are typically planted in the United States and then send missionaries back home to evangelize the unreached there. Asian churches and Asian seminaries in the United States also provide resources to build theological schools in Asia as a way to train indigenous Christian leaders for the future. As I mentioned in chapter 1, Logos Seminary founded another seminary in Taiwan to equip Christian leaders to serve the needs of the people there. In recent years, Logos also launched an Asian Ministry Center, which sends faculty and qualified alumni to teach at multiple sites in Asia. It equips local Chinese Christian leaders for ministry and for the work of building up their own networks for theological education that is both biblical and contextual. Reaching out to the Chinese diaspora has been Logos's missional effort in responding to EFC's denominational vision of church planting and evangelism. However, the EFC denomination also ministers to people of other races and ethnicities. For example, EFC has planted a church in Central America called EFC Belize, whose congregation includes local Spanish-speaking and English-speaking Christians. A few EFC churches also employ people of non-Chinese descent to be pastors of their congregations.

As Christianity gradually declines in the West, it is becoming increasingly vibrant in Asia and throughout the Chinese diaspora. I believe Asia will be one of the strong waves that will shape the future of theological education, whether by an increase in students from Asia or through Chinese programs. It is up to the theological schools to decide whether they want to catch that wave. The increase in Asian seminaries as well as the soaring number of Christians in China who desire theological education reflect a missiological wave that will continue to surge into the future of theological education.

Pneumatology

The increasing presence of Asian seminaries in general and the thriving of Logos Seminary in particular demonstrate the work of the Spirit in theological education between the times. As early as 900 BCE, the prophet Joel prophesied concerning the "Day of the LORD":

> It will come about after this
> That I will pour out My Spirit on all mankind;
> And your sons and daughters will prophesy,
> Your old men will dream dreams,
> Your young men will see visions.
> Even on the male and female servants
> I will pour out My Spirit in those days. (Joel 2:28–29)

From Joel's vantage point, in the distant future there will come a time when God will pour out his Spirit on "all mankind." Joel then defined "all mankind" as three sets of people: sons and daughters, old men and young men, and male and female servants. In the distant future, the Spirit of God will not be reserved only for the male but will be available for the female as well. The support of women in ministry at Logos Seminary is a pragmatic recognition of gifts for ministry and an ethical commitment to gender equality. But it is also more than this. It is a sign of the realization of Joel's vision.

"The Day of the LORD" that Joel prophesied finds its fulfillment on the Day of Pentecost, on which people with different tongues/languages gathered together in one place. As they gathered, a noise like a violent rushing wind filled the place, they saw tongues of fire descending, they were all filled with the Holy Spirit, and each spoke with tongues about the mighty deeds of God that others would understand (Acts 2:1–11). While Joel prophesied that God would pour out his Spirit on all people, the Pentecost story indicates that one of the manifestations of the Spirit is speaking in other tongues. Theological schools that use the students' native tongue—whether it be Mandarin, Korean, or Spanish—as the instructional language provide a further example of this manifestation of the Spirit, namely, that the Spirit does not discriminate, that all people who profess Jesus as Lord belong to the people of God. The inclusiveness as well as the comprehensiveness of this people of God point to the kingdom of God that welcomes people of all races, ethnicities, and tongues. In this sense, the presence of diasporic theological schools is a welcome phenomenon when viewed from the perspective of pneumatology. Through the rise of diasporic seminaries, God is doing a new thing and redefining who his people are.

Contextualization

I have a Chinese friend who enrolled in the PhD program of an English-speaking seminary and majored in practical theology. I asked him one day how he was getting on at his seminary, and he said he felt frustrated, not because of the language barrier but because of the cultural differences. He mentioned that most

of his professors were Caucasians. When they discussed ministry contexts in class, they would cite examples or case studies
based on predominantly white American churches. All the lecture materials came from a white perspective. As a member of
an immigrant church, my friend found this disconcerting. What
he learned in class and from the assigned readings was not appli-
cable to his own ministry context, which is a Chinese immigrant
church with three congregations, worshiping in three different
languages, with generational and cultural gaps between the first-
and second-generation Chinese. A white-oriented ministry road-
map simply does not fit well in a context and culture different
from that white paradigm. At the root of my friend's complaints
was that the paradigm for ministry taught at his seminary was
thoroughly white. Contextualization meant nothing beyond
white experience. Willie Jennings's book in the series speaks
precisely against this "white model as the standard model" in
theological education.

The presence of diasporic communities would help meet this
doctoral student's need for contextualization. In fact, contextualization may well be one of the significant reasons for establishing
ethnic and diasporic seminaries. In the world of ministry, "one
size does not fit all." One of the benefits of attending a seminary
like Logos is that it prepares students to serve more effectively
in the cultural context in which they find themselves. If there is
a formula for contextual theology, it would be "local + global =
contextual."[16] For instance, Logos Seminary offers courses such
as "Chinese Church History," "Asian American Ministry," and
other practical theology courses that specifically address the
needs of Chinese immigrant churches. It also offers courses in
missions and intercultural studies, providing a global perspective of the kingdom of God. The language the student is using
is the same language the student would use in future ministry.
The professors are familiar with the Chinese church context and
would integrate their knowledge of ministry better than someone
from a different culture. Most students at Logos form networks
of relationships with the people they encounter while pursuing

theological education. These relational networks prove beneficial in their future ministries in the Chinese contexts as well. Therefore, there is a need for ethnic and diasporic seminaries that the mainstream English-speaking seminaries presently cannot meet.

A few years ago, my dissertation adviser, John Goldingay, invited me to present a paper at the Biblical Colloquium at Fuller Theological Seminary. My paper was later published as "Reading Job as a Chinese Diasporian."[17] Students of many different nationalities and ethnicities had a place at the conference-room table, listening and engaging as I presented the paper. After the presentation, a Hispanic student came up to me and expressed his appreciation that although I was writing from the perspective of a Chinese person in the Chinese diaspora, a lot of what I had discovered from the intersection between the biblical text and my own social location spoke to him and his Hispanic diasporic experience. He came from Fuller's Hispanic program, normally conducted in Spanish. Here we were, two people from different ethnicities who belonged to different diasporic communities but who felt we were connected in the same spirit and shared similar social contexts. Contextualization requires getting specific. But it does not have to be isolating. Sometimes the best way to connect with others is by attending carefully to one's own context.

Diasporic seminaries and the presence of diasporic communities contribute to missiology, pneumatology, and contextualization. This expands the kingdom of God while at the same time nuancing it. Meanwhile, diasporic seminaries that serve a diasporic student body also have their own set of challenges. In what follows, I address these challenges according to two aspects: internal forces and external forces.

Challenges Due to Internal Forces

Internal challenges in diasporic seminaries can be related to instructional language, racial diversity, and problems associated with future generations of diasporic students.

Instructional Language

On one hand, using one's native tongue as the instructional language improves educational effectiveness. Students no longer experience a language barrier in their learning process. On the other hand, using a non-English language as the instructional language generates other concerns. Logos Seminary, located in Los Angeles, uses Mandarin as its instructional language, training Chinese students to minister in the Chinese diaspora. Students may be well versed in Chinese and familiar with the Chinese context, but this comes at the expense of learning English and integrating English into their ministry and life. The lack of English proficiency restricts them in actual ministry contexts, given that most immigrant churches have a second-generation ministry that is English-speaking only. More and more immigrant Chinese churches conduct their pastoral meetings in English and record meeting minutes in English because their English-speaking pastor does not understand the Chinese language. The lack of English proficiency also hinders students from integrating into broader American society. That said, most international or immigrant students attending theological school in the United States do not intend to integrate into American society but desire to serve at a local ethnic church.

It is also extremely difficult for a seminary like Logos to hire qualified bilingual faculty. Because all faculty members need to have a command of Mandarin and English, applicants who do not speak Mandarin are automatically disqualified. While mainstream seminaries have too many applicants for the very few vacant positions, Logos Seminary often has more faculty positions available than viable candidates to fill them.

As regards research and publication, most faculty members at Logos publish in Chinese, serving the needs of Chinese Christians globally. Yet the English-speaking world is not aware of these publications, and this may project the image that Chinese seminaries are doing their own thing or are confined to their own ethnic and theological enclave and that their faculty's publications have no relevance for the larger academic world, specifically the English-speaking world. While Logos's faculty's writings may address the needs of the Chinese ecclesial and theological communities, there remains a greater challenge: to be relevant to the mainstream academy. And since Logos is situated in North America and not in Asia, that mainstream academy is English speaking. The only remedy to this challenge seems to be to encourage publication in English alongside Chinese, so as to remain visible and relevant to the larger ecclesial and academic communities. Yet not all faculty members have the time and energy to write in both languages.

Last but not least, establishing Mandarin as the instructional language also creates a culture that tends to reinforce Chinese identity at the expense of Christian identity that embraces diversity and inclusivity. God's people incorporate all races, ethnicities, and languages. Limiting the instructional language to one tends to limit the global nature of the kingdom of God, in practice if not in conception. The same applies to using English as the instructional language. God's kingdom does not belong only to those who speak English, nor only to those who speak Mandarin, but to people from all nations and all tongues. Therefore there exists a tension between using Mandarin as an instructional language and expressing diversity and the global nature of God's kingdom. A plurality of languages in theological education is a worthy goal to pursue and embrace. I explore this subject further in the next chapter.

Racial Diversity

Along with the limitations of using one's ethnic language as the instructional language comes the issue of racial diversity. The cultural roots of Logos Seminary originate in the Taiwanese immigrants in the Los Angeles area. For its first twenty years, it progressed steadily in cultural diversity. The former academic dean of Logos Seminary, Ekron Chen, has traced this progression as follows:[18]

Figure 2.3. Diversity at Logos Seminary, 1989–2008

Year	Cultural Milestones at Logos Seminary
1989	The founding of the seminary, using Taiwanese as the instructional language; faculty and students are all of Taiwanese descent
1994	First non-Taiwanese student enrolled (from China)
1995	First non-Chinese student enrolled (a Korean)
2002	First English Asian American course offered
2005	First time that TOEFL[19] scores were required from students who have not earned a degree in English
2007	Logos's Chinese name realigned from "Tai-Fu" to "Zheng-Dao"
2008	First non-Chinese faculty member hired (an American missionary)

The highest point in faculty diversity was reached in 2011, with the hiring of another non-Chinese faculty person, this one also an American missionary. Two other faculty members who were born and raised in China also joined our faculty in 2013 and 2014, respectively. In 2019 to 2020, the percentage of non-Chinese faculty at Logos was 15 percent. The seminary has made progress, but it still has room to grow in its racial and cultural diversity.

Ten years ago, Chen identified three challenges regarding diversity at Logos. He noted that (1) student diversity seems to have plateaued; (2) Logos is still overwhelmingly Chinese; and (3) progress toward bilingualism is slow due to the current lack of resources to build a two-track curriculum that includes courses in both Chinese and English.[20] Ten years after Chen's article, more than 60 percent of the students have a Chinese background. Whereas in the first two decades of Logos 70 percent of students were from Taiwan or of Taiwanese descent, now the majority have a Chinese background. Today, Logos is still primarily although not exclusively Chinese, given the appointment of two American former missionaries to the faculty (although one of them stepped down in July 2019).

Diversity of language and ethnicity *within* Logos is important because the school is committed to preparing students for ministry in immigrant Chinese churches and in cross-cultural missions that are increasingly bi- and trilingual. But even with limited internal diversity, Logos, like all diasporic seminaries, makes a significant contribution to the diversity of the larger world of theological education precisely through its relatively homogenous ethnicity. But it is still important to diversify diasporic seminaries internally, so that students can learn from students and faculty of different races, ethnicities, and cultures.

Next Generations

Since Logos is using Mandarin as its instructional language and since a majority of its students are either immigrants or international students, there exists a discontinuity between the first-generation Chinese-speaking students and the second-generation English-speaking Chinese community. Most Chinese immigrant churches in the United States have more than one congregation. The children of the first-generation immigrants tend to go to the English service and worship in English. Their first-generation parents tend to go to either Mandarin, Taiwanese, or Cantonese services. Most graduates from Logos would have a difficult time adjusting to the immigrant Chinese church context, particularly engaging the English-speaking congregation. The problem has to do not only with the difference in language but also with the difference in culture. Take food, for example. First-generation Chinese immigrants are accustomed to eating pig feet as a dish. The fatty skin is considered nutritious and a good source of collagen. However, their second-generation children consider this "offensive." If a seminary speaks in only one language and studies in a monocultural context, how will its students reach out to those English-speaking generations with a different culture, be they second or third generation?

External Forces

We will discuss two external factors affecting diasporic seminaries: the political climate of China and the rise of other
Chinese seminaries.

The China Factor

Since a large number of students at Logos Seminary hold visas from
China, the changing nature of China's politics and its regulations
affects enrollment rather directly. A number of times in recent
years, half of the admitted students from China have been denied
visas. With the tightening of religious policy in China since 2018,
the future of China as a source of students will be contingent on this
"China Factor." This factor will also influence strategies for recruiting future students from China. A diasporic school like Logos may
not be able to recruit its core student body from mainland China
but may have to look elsewhere or utilize online programs.

The Rise of Other Chinese Seminaries

Logos Seminary is an emerging seminary that is flourishing
amidst both the challenges and possibilities for theological education between the times. While Logos is the first ATS-accredited
theological school that uses Mandarin as its instructional language, it is not the only school of its kind. More and more Chinese seminaries are becoming ATS member schools. In addition,
new Chinese programs are being launched in California and elsewhere in the United States at English-speaking seminaries such
as Dallas Theological Seminary, Gordon-Conwell Theological
Seminary, and Midwestern Baptist Theological Seminary, all of
which have Chinese programs. With the rise of Christianity in
China, this trend is likely to continue well into the future.

In Los Angeles alone, there are at least six other Chinese seminaries or seminaries with a Chinese program: China Evangelical
Seminary North America, Truth Theological Seminary, Global

Enrichment Theological Seminary, Chinese for Christ Calvin Chao Theological Seminary, Global Life Enrichment Center, and Gateway Seminary. Fuller Seminary's China Initiative also aims to launch a full-fledged Chinese program in the future. In northern California, there are several Chinese seminaries as well, including Christian Witness Theological Seminary, Christian Leadership Institute, and Relevant Theological Institute. In Flushing, New York, there is a Faith Bible Association, which offers courses and confers degrees. On Canada's west coast is Tyndale Theological College, with Chinese programs in both English and Chinese. On the East Coast, Carey Theological College has a Chinese program that includes both Mandarin and Cantonese tracks.

With such a "cloud of witnesses" of the Chinese seminaries and programs, the challenge of running a Chinese seminary or a Chinese program in North America is paramount. In light of this "friendly competition," improving educational quality and effectiveness will determine the success or failure of each institution at offering appropriate theological education between the times.

Concluding Reflections

In this chapter, I have identified seven areas in which the story of Logos Seminary serves as a counternarrative to stories usually told about theological education. These are signs of the times within the landscape of theological education in North America and around the globe, specifically signaling that there are diasporic communities and seminaries that exist to form Christians for God's global church. Theological education is not limited to the main narratives in the West that are structured by a polarity of white and black. Instead, there is a whole range of multiethnic, diasporic, transnational students out there doing God's kingdom work in ways that appear to be "hidden in plain sight." Logos Seminary has been located on US soil for thirty years. It has been transforming Chinese Christianity not just in the United States but globally. That more and more immigrants and people with diasporic identity become Christians here in the United States creates a need for immigrant and diasporic churches and pastors who minister to them. The influence of diasporic seminaries like Logos may seem hidden in the eyes of the dominant culture, but it is always visible in the eyes of God.

I believe that Logos and other diasporic seminaries have things to offer wider conversations about theological education. If the formation model of education is deemed a significant shift in Christian higher education, perhaps the West can learn from the East and from schools such as Logos Seminary where that model has been at the core of its educational philosophy since its inception. The primacy of spiritual formation at Logos has to be credited to Felix Liu's philosophy of theological education that has shaped both the curriculum of master's-level degree programs and extracurricular activities such as weekly prayer meetings and fasts. These spiritual practices are ingrained in the Chinese Christian spiritual traditions as well as in other Chinese seminaries in Asia. Logos's stresses on the formational model may inform other theological schools about its merits and limits. For example, students living in the seminary dorm would learn to relate to other students and their families in a communal way. Living together in a close community helps students to acquire relational competence that classroom education may not be able to offer. However, living in such a tight Chinese Christian community may prevent students from learning in a larger, cross-cultural setting and thus limits their exposure to people from other races and cultures.

The focus on forming servants rather than leaders may invite dialogue on the goal of theological education. If the goal of theological schools is to form future leaders, then we need to define the qualities and character traits of these leaders. Are we to form those who only lead but don't serve or those who only serve but don't lead (or are unable to lead), or leaders who both lead and serve? How do we strive to form servant-leaders who are not too arrogant to serve or too timid to lead?

If the instructional language is a tool for all people to know

God, then should we privilege one language over another? In the global context of theological education, should there be more theological schools that use Spanish, Korean, Cantonese, or Vietnamese as the instructional language, and should not publications in all languages be welcomed and celebrated?

The special status of the MDiv degree at Logos and its involvement in assessing the fitness of applicants reflect Logos's strong commitment to shaping future pastors, not just general Christian workers in diverse ministries. Though there are changes afoot in the practices of theological education, certain essential core values and practices endure the test of time, values such as the sacredness of the call to full-time pastoral ministry, and the theological school as well as the ecclesial community's recognition and support of that call.

The support of women in ministry and leadership has not been widely practiced in evangelical Protestant schools largely due to theological conviction and denominational traditions. The Logos model of seeing both women and men as equal partners in ministry reflects the seminary's openness to the leading of the Holy Spirit and the seminary's vision of the kingdom of God as inclusive. This counternarrative speaks boldly to other evangelical Protestant schools as well as Asian and Asian American churches about what it means to live out the gospel in a patriarchal context.

While financing theological education is increasingly an individual responsibility in the West, the Chinese culture is always communal, including in the area of finance. Students at Logos have various opportunities to receive financial support, through the EFC denomination, their own church denomination or church mission department, or friends and family. In the Chinese Christian contexts, going to seminary and into ministry is perceived as a higher calling that deserves communal support. Perhaps the West might consider the benefits of perceiving theological education as a communal effort rather than an individual matter.

Last but not least, the launching of the PhD program at Logos for the future of theological education in the Chinese di-

aspora may encourage more theological schools to look beyond their own generation to future generations of students
and to encourage more schools to engage in global but also
contextual theologies.

Through these counternarratives, Logos has something to
contribute to further these conversations. It is evident that diasporic seminaries will become increasingly visible in the future
as more Asian seminaries become ATS member schools and as
more theological schools launch their own Chinese (and other
language) programs. In the grand narrative of God's kingdom,
people from different tribes, races, ethnicities, and tongues
will be included as one people, as Revelation 7:9–10 envisions.
Therefore, one of the goals of theological education must be to
shape students toward this kingdom perspective, building together an educational model that exemplifies diversity in unity
and unity in diversity. There is a place for diasporic schools and
ethnic programs in the future of theological education as long
as they do not exist at the expense of diversity, which is at the
very heart of God. What does diversity really mean in a diasporic
context? To this prospect of redefining diversity we turn in our
next chapter.

Redefining Diversity in the Diaspora

A few years ago, an African American professor who served as an ATS liaison came to Logos Seminary for a focus visit. Because our mission statement mentions that we encourage diversity, he asked whether someone like him could study at Logos; "diversity" would imply that he could. Our response to him was that by "diversity" we mean diversity in the Chinese context. That is, we welcome students of any race, class, and gender *who can understand Mandarin*—the common language of the Chinese people (and the most spoken language on the planet, a language that crosses national and ethnic borders). In the cultural context of the United States, when a school uses Mandarin as the instructional language and when its students are mostly Chinese, it may understandably not seem diverse. But in the global context of Logos Seminary, the use of Mandarin actually transcends race and ethnicity since it *welcomes people of any race and ethnicity* to learn together as a global community. In short, the understanding of diversity is different depending on one's cultural context.

Demographers predict that by 2040 people of color will outnumber Caucasians in the United States.[1] With the rise of diasporic seminaries such as Logos Evangelical Seminary and other Chinese programs in theological schools between the times, and with increasing plurality and diversity in the practices of theological education, each institution will need not only to embrace diversity but also to redefine it according to its mission and social location.

As we interact with Scripture in this chapter, we will see that God prefers diversity over homogeneity, plurality over singularity, and unity in multiplicity. At the same time, there is a place for the kind of shared community made possible with a kind of homogeneity and particularity. The full realization of the kingdom of God includes people of all nations, tribes, ethnicities, languages, and cultures. However, for now we are in the "already but not yet" stage, wrestling with interconnectedness among diversity, justice, and unity. This chapter interacts with Scripture on the issues of diaspora, language, and culture from Babel to the book of Revelation and then reassesses what I understand by diversity in light of the particularity of Logos Evangelical Seminary. As we will see, the existence of this seminary is largely a result of the dispersion of people from China to the rest of the globe. For whatever reason, Chinese people were dispersed, and whether that dispersion was from China to Taiwan or from China all the way to the United States, I understand dispersion both in biblical times and now as one of the ways to bring about the kingdom of God. Therefore, dispersion exerts its positive impact on the grand narrative of God's mission.

The year 2019 marked the thirtieth anniversary of Logos Seminary. In response to the new era, Logos's president, Kuo Liang Lin, led the whole school in revisiting the school's mission statement. The process involved major stakeholders of the seminary community. Although many issues were discussed, we talked especially about whether we should include spiritual formation in the mission statement, since spiritual formation has been a distinctive emphasis of the school since its founding. We also discussed whether we should include holistic formation of students in the mission statement, since the former mission statement named four things the seminary intended to equip students in: spiritual formation, academic excellence, ministerial competency, and godly living. At the end of the process, it came down to one issue: whether the mission statement should include the word "Chinese." While the inclusion of "Chinese" would spell out our distinction as a diasporic seminary, the term also seems to limit the school's mission, which is always global. The inclusion of the ethnic marker "Chinese" highlights Logos's distinction from other American seminaries, but it also seems to deny racial and ethnic diversity and is contrary to the seminary's intent to be missional and global. The tension of whether to include "Chinese" in the new mission statement persisted among Logos's leadership and faculty for several months, until the president gave the final decision to the seminary board. After deliberation, the board decided to omit "Chinese" from the mission statement, thus fully endorsing the global mission of Logos. Therefore, the existence of Logos Seminary and other diasporic seminaries suggests that there is an urgent need to redefine diversity.

The Diversity of Languages in Babel

In discussions on biblical views of language and ethnicity, the story of Babel always comes to mind. Is the plurality of languages a curse or a blessing? Does God delight in the plurality of languages? What does dispersion mean to the future of theological education? With these questions in mind, let us reexamine the story of Babel in Genesis 11:1–9:

> Now the whole earth used the same language and the same words. It came about as they journeyed east, that they found a plain in the land of Shinar and settled there. They said to one another, "Come, let us make bricks and burn them thoroughly." And they used brick for stone, and they used tar for mortar. They said, "Come, let us build for ourselves a city, and a tower whose top will reach into heaven, and let us make for ourselves a name, otherwise we will be scattered abroad over the face of the whole earth." The LORD came down to see the city and the tower which the sons of men had built. The LORD said, "Behold, they are one people, and they all have the same language. And this is what they

began to do, and now nothing which they purpose to do will be impossible for them. Come, let Us go down and there confuse their language, so that they will not understand one another's speech." So the LORD scattered them abroad from there over the face of the whole earth; and they stopped building the city. Therefore its name was called Babel, because there the LORD confused the language of the whole earth; and from there the LORD scattered them abroad over the face of the whole earth.

Interpretations of the story of Babel vary widely. Some scholars understand the text to describe the origin of different cultures and languages; some regard the multiplicity of language as divine punishment for human hubris or sin.[2] By contrast, others regard the diverse languages as reflecting God's preference for diversity,[3] and still others read the story ideologically as a text against the Babylonian Empire and, by implication, against contemporary empires such as the United States.[4] Others interpret the dispersion of people with different languages as a curse and the event of Pentecost (at which people spoke different languages yet could still understand each other) as the antidote to or redemption of Babel.[5] There are others still who understand the story in the larger context of shattering the image of God and restoring that image through the election of Israel.[6]

I see an echo of the story of Babel in the history of ancient China during its first imperial dynasty—the Qin Dynasty. The Qin Dynasty was quite short-lived, lasting only fifteen years, from 221 to 206 BCE, but its impact on the subsequent culture of China has been enduring. Qin Shi Huang (which means "the first emperor") is most well known for his armies of human-sized terracotta warriors unearthed in the province of Xi An in 1974. This underground terra-cotta army reflects Qin's desire to build an empire even after his death. Another crowning achievement of Qin was his unification of China through one language and one script—Mandarin. At a time when China was composed of multiple provinces with people speaking in different dialects, the unification through one language and one script enhanced commercial and political undertakings and changed life in China forever. Qin intended to build an empire by forcing local provinces to learn the same language and the same script. Qin perceived the existence of a variety of languages in one country as a barrier to the centralization of power and unification of China. Eventually, Qin succeeded in the unification of China through his military campaigns and through reforms such as standardizing currency, weights, measures, and a single system of writing.[7]

On the surface, his scheme of centralization did indeed forge unity. Yet, this forced unity also diminished diversity across the nation. His underlying assumption (and that of many people since) is that diversity promotes decentralization and thus disunity. Qin's endeavor to unify China reflects his agenda to hoard power for himself. Such political unification undermines cultural diversity and creativity. People speaking different languages thus became an obstacle to Qin's plans to unify China. Qin's ambition resembles that of the people at Babel, who desired to build a city and a tower in order to prevent their dispersal. At the core of their thinking and of Qin's was domination through forced unification. Even in his death, Qin's craving for that power is evident to the world in the form of the massed terra-cotta warriors.

Given the stories of Babel and Qin, is speaking different languages a curse? What is wrong with centralization? Does God not prefer unification? To understand the story of Babel in Genesis 11 fully, I suggest that we read it in light of its close affinity with the Table of Nations in Genesis 10 and the call of Abraham in Genesis 12:1–3.

Genesis 11:1–9 has several key terms in common with Genesis 10, which suggests their literary connections, as shown in figure 3.1 below:

Figure 3.1. *Common vocabulary in Genesis 10 and 11:1–9*

Key terms	Genesis 10	Genesis 11:1–9
Shinar (*Shinar*)	10:10	11:1
Scatter (*putz*)	10:18	11:4, 8, 9

Key terms	Genesis 10	Genesis 11:1–9
Build (*banah*)	10:11	11:4, 5, 8
Land (*eretz*)	10:5, 20, 31–32	11:1, 8, 9
Language/tongue/lip (*lashon*)	10:5, 20, 31	11:1, 6, 7, 9
Name/Shem (*shem*)[8]	10:1, 21, 22, 31	11:4, 10, 11

A dominant literary as well as theological connection throughout Genesis 10–12 is the idea of dispersion and centralization. The spreading of the people in the land was part of God's charge to Noah and his sons: "Be fruitful and multiply, and fill the earth" (Gen. 9:1). This charge reiterates the same command given to humankind when God created it (Gen. 1:28). Reading the Table of Nations in this larger framework suggests that the dispersion of the people was not the consequence of divine judgment. Rather, it was the divine intention all along. Dispersion implies diversity, multiplicity, and localization, which are inherited in God's creation. People divided into separate ethnic groups, each group with its own language and culture. The dispersion of those groups offers a ready way in which to propagate the kingdom of God. In the early church, people were dispersed due to persecution, but the kingdom of God expanded as a result of the dispersion. The presence of Logos Evangelical Seminary, a Chinese diasporic seminary in the United States, can be understood as part of this broader process of dispersion for the kingdom of God.

For political and economic reasons, many Chinese were dispersed into other parts of the world in the early twentieth century. Since then, Chinese have been present in all corners of the planet. Consequently, the Chinese in the Chinese diaspora are as diverse in culture and language as it is possible to be. The Chinese from Singapore and Malaysia are different from the Chinese from China or Taiwan—in national history, in culture, in food, and in language. For instance, many Chinese from Singapore speak English with a Singaporean accent. Some of them mix Mandarin and English together to form their own "Singalish." The British colonial occupation also gave Singaporeans a close affinity with the Western world. By contrast, the Chinese in Malaysia are often multilingual, speaking Mandarin, Cantonese, Malay, and Malaysian English. Since their ancestors relocated from China to Malaysia, the later generations of Chinese in Malaysia have struggled with their sense of identity, as they are neither the "real" Chinese, who live in China, nor the native Malaysians, whose only country is Malaysia. The Chinese from China itself also display remarkable diversity since each of the approximately thirty provinces in China boasts its own culture and dialects. People from each province differentiate their ethnicity from that of other provinces. Thus, among the Chinese people there are Shanghainese, Fujianese, Hakka people, Shandong people, Guangzhao people, and so forth. We may therefore say that being Chinese is being diverse.

Differences in food begin to suggest the broader differences in culture. The Chinese from the north prefer noodles and dumplings, whereas the Chinese from the south see rice as their staple, their "bread and butter." The Chinese from Taiwan are also complicated. Some relocated from China to Taiwan in the mid-twentieth century, while those born in Taiwan as Chinese are not considered native Taiwanese. There are also the indigenous Taiwanese, whose outward appearance, culture, and language can differ substantially from prevailing notions of what counts as Chinese. In much the same way, although Logos *seems* to be homogenous in race (as the majority of faculty, staff, and students are Chinese), the seminary is actually quite diverse as a result of the variety of ethnicities, cultures, and dialects present on campus.

Genesis 10–11 is not the end of the story. God called Abraham out of Ur, the land of Shem, so that through Abraham "all the families of the earth will be blessed" (Gen. 12:3). God affirmed centralization in one person, and through him God anticipated another dispersion of families—only this time for the purpose of blessing them. In this sense, the dispersion of Noah's families in Genesis 10 finds its *telos* in God's intention to bless all the families of the earth through Abraham. The purpose of centralization is dispersion, and the purpose of dispersion is to bring blessings to all. Since the creation of the world, God's intention has been to bless.

It is through this larger context of blessing and cursing that we read Genesis 10–11. The story of Babel demonstrates the downward spiral of sin and its manifestations in humans' centralization rather than humans dispersing and filling the earth as bearers of God's image and as those who reign in his stead. In other words, Babel is the antithesis of God's creational purpose. The problem of human centralization and single language is not a sin in and of itself; the sin comes in exalting a human-centered agenda. This human-centered agenda is manifested in the people of Babel, who, through making a name for themselves and through building a city and a tower, try to avoid dispersion. The prophet Zephaniah envisioned an eschatological future in which people speak with purified lips, and in which all call on the name of God (Zeph. 3:9). This portrait of centralization reflects an idealized future in which humanity will speak with one voice to proclaim God's name—rather than their own name, as they did at Babel, where people desired to make a name for themselves (Gen. 11:4). Therefore, the diversification of language at Babel is not simply the result of the curse but a means to extend the kingdom of God.

A Case for Plurality of Languages

The diversity of race and ethnicity as expressed by the sons of Noah demonstrates God's preference for diversity over homogeneity. If the world is God's temple, he desires his reign to reach every corner of the earth. He desires the image, and thus the knowledge, of him to permeate the entire globe. When human beings fill the earth through dispersion, it is the first step in furthering that reign. Yet theological education in North America is dominated by English, while European languages such as German and French are esteemed and expected for research in the theological fields. Other languages such as Spanish, Chinese, or

Korean are deemed "sublanguages," even if not explicitly named as such. Sometimes the dominant group (the English group) judges the academic competence of the other groups (such as immigrants) by how well they speak and write English, by how well they conform to the way English is supposed to be spoken by Americans, as well as by whether they think and argue in a Western way and with Western eloquence. The sense of superiority of the dominant group is evident in academia, in classrooms, and in social settings. Since language is inseparable from culture and power, the dominance of the English language in North America suggests where the dominant culture lies and where power resides. Regarding the politics of language, Indonesian American scholar Ekaputra Tupamahu writes about the challenges to "decolonize English" by not submitting oneself to a dominant colonial language or speaking like a native English speaker. The essence of his study lies precisely in the direct correlation between language and power.[9]

Although most Chinese speak Mandarin, many are bilingual, trilingual, or multilingual owing to their various social locations, cultures, and experiences. For example, some Chinese speak Mandarin and Cantonese, while others speak multiple Asian languages, such as Mandarin, Cantonese, Malaysian, and Fujianese. My parents speak Mandarin, Cantonese, and Vietnamese, and their lives are mingled with all three cultures. Many people from Taiwan speak both Mandarin and Taiwanese. An example of the interrelationship between culture and language is how the Chinese people in different countries say the word "Mandarin"—the common spoken Chinese language. For Singaporeans, Mandarin is "Hua Wen." People from Taiwan refer to Mandarin as "Guo Yu" or "Hua Yu." People from China say "Pu Tong Hua." All have the same meaning but use a different vocabulary. Simply hearing how a person says the word "Mandarin" (in his or her language) can reveal a lot about the person's country of origin and culture. So when a Chinese person addresses another group of Chinese people by using their preferred word for "Mandarin," it reflects respect for the other group's cultures and identities.

While the Chinese are mostly one race but are also multilingual and multicultural, Americans speak mostly one language but are of many races. Each culture displays diversity in its own way. The kingdom of God includes people of all nations and a plurality of languages. The dominant group and the minoritized groups are both part of the community of the people of God. One is not superior to the other. One race can be perceived as homogenous, just like one language may appear to lack any kind of diversity. Most immigrant churches have at least two and sometimes three languages, whereas American churches typically speak in only one language, although their members may be of many races. Most Americans have only one hometown, whereas in the Chinese diasporic context, people have multiple hometowns. Diversity happens in different ways in different cultures. There is a diversity of diversities.

Theological education needs to reflect this diversity—not just to accommodate students, but to know God truly. By definition, theological education centers on the study of God, since in Latin *theo* means God and *logos* refers to "the study of." Therefore, knowing God has to be a *telos*, or end and meaning of theological education, if not the sole *telos*. In his inspiring work *Knowing God*, J. I. Packer distinguishes "knowledge about God" from "knowledge of God." He suggests that in order to turn the knowledge about God into knowledge of God, one needs to turn each truth that one learns about God into meditation before God, which then leads to prayer and praise to God.[10] For only when the knowledge of God reaches every corner of the earth will the reign of God be realized on the earth. Since all people are created in the image of God and all people are descended from the sons of Noah and their wives, who populated the world in their own languages and regions as portrayed in Genesis 10, the image of God includes people of all races, ethnicities, and languages. No one race or ethnicity should claim a monopoly as the sole reflection of the image of God or as the only race that expresses the knowledge of God.

If knowing God is the *telos* of theological education, then the language to bring about that knowledge serves merely as a means to an end. Diasporic and ethnic theological schools where instruction occurs in different languages, be it Mandarin, Cantonese, Korean, or Spanish, reflect people of diverse cultures who are learning and teaching in their own native languages to bring the knowledge of God to their own people, so that they can all be God's representatives and spread his image to every corner of the earth. In light of this theological understanding, diasporic theological schools or ethnic programs reflect a global perspective of theological education rather than existing as marginal schools among ATS schools or in the broader spectrum of theological schools. Those who hold the view that Eurocentric mainline Protestant schools are the center of theological education may very well become the "new Babel" without realizing it. A plurality of languages in theological education reflects the wider community of the people of God, which should be promoted rather than repressed or subjugated under the dominant language or race. Although one common language would facilitate communication among people of different languages, that common language should not be equated with the "best" language or the most powerful language on the earth. It should be instead a *lingua franca*, a vehicle to transmit knowledge and not a tool to dominate others. Since language reflects diversity and culture, a plurality of languages in theological education enables one culture to learn from another, which is not only a theological virtue but also a theological necessity, affirming the multiplicity and the inclusivity of the kingdom of God.

From Abraham to the Pentecost

At the end of Genesis 11 is the genealogy of Shem, the chosen son of Noah, because out of Shem came Abraham. As the descendants of Shem dispersed according to their own families, languages, lands, and nations in the region of Mesopotamia (Gen. 10:31), God called Abraham from there to the land that he would show him. God said to Abraham:

"Go forth from your country
And from your relatives
And from your father's house,
To the land which I will show you;
And I will make you a great nation,
And I will bless you,
And make your name great;
And so you shall be a blessing;
And I will bless those who bless you,
And the one who curses you I will curse.
And in you all the families of the earth will be blessed."

(Gen. 12:1–3)

Through the call of Abraham, God intervened in human history and rewrote it. Three short verses have reshaped the direction of human history since then. Some deem these verses to be the center of the Old Testament. For example, in his *Theology of the Book of Genesis*, R. W. L. Moberly regards the assurance of blessing to Abraham in Genesis 12:1–3 as a key to interpreting the whole Old Testament.[11] Old Testament scholar and missiologist Christopher J. H. Wright considers Genesis 12:1–3 a "pivotal text" that functions as a hermeneutical key to the grand narrative of the mission of God. The entire missional narrative in the Old Testament is about God's blessing going from Abraham to the nations.[12] By calling Abraham, God intended that through Abraham all the families of the earth would be blessed (Gen. 12:3) in the sense that they would all know God. The families that were dispersed in Genesis 10 found their connection once again in the call of Abraham. The new people of God are identified in Abraham. This renewed centralization forms a direct contrast to the centralization of Babel, where people wanted to make a name for themselves. Instead, it is God who will make the name of Abraham great (Gen. 12:2).

This God is a God who both blesses and curses. Those who side with Abraham will be blessed, and those who disparage him will be cursed (Gen. 12:3). Dispersion and centralization have their respective places in the grand narrative of Scripture. Through Abraham, all the families of the earth will be blessed. These families point backward to the families of the sons of Noah in Genesis 10, but at the same time, they point forward to the future families of the people of God. Through one person (centralization), the families of the global village (dispersion) will be blessed. The current landscape of the Chinese diaspora and the Hispanic diaspora illustrates the consequence of dispersion and contributes to the yellowing as well as the browning of Christianity in the global village.

However, the dispersion of the people at Babel, which caused the confusion of language as well as the calling of Abraham as a blessing to the families of the earth, is only part of the story. A new development occurred over two thousand years later on the Day of Pentecost when Jews and gentiles were all gathered together in one place (Acts 2:1). Theologian Willie Jennings calls this event "the epicenter of the revolution" and "the revolution of the intimate" because of the disrupting presence of the Spirit of God.[13] Then and there, something unexpected exploded: "When the day of Pentecost had come, they were all together in one place. And suddenly there came from heaven a noise like a violent rushing wind, and it filled the whole house where they were sitting. And there appeared to them tongues as of fire distributing themselves, and they rested on each one of them. And they were all filled with the Holy Spirit and began to speak with other tongues, as the Spirit was giving them utterance" (Acts 2:1–4).

A theophany with the presence of wind, fire, and loud noise occurred on the Day of Pentecost. The event was reminiscent of the theophany on Mount Sinai when God descended upon it, with smoke ascending like the smoke of a furnace. The mountain quaked violently, the sound of the trumpet grew louder and louder, and the voice of God was like thunder (Exod. 19:18–19). This time, it was the Holy Spirit who descended and filled the audience. The descent of "tongues of fire" indicates a theophany (Isa. 5:24–25; 30:27–30). In this case it manifested in persons speaking in languages other than their own but everyone understanding one another. Jennings vividly describes this speaking in tongues: "This is God touching, taking hold of tongue and voice, mind, heart, and body. This is a joining, unprecedented, unanticipated, unwanted, yet complete joining."[14] While the disciples anticipated the power of God descending on them, the speaking of one another's language was a complete surprise. Jennings calls this a "real grace," which contrasts with the human ambition to have power over others and instead stresses God's desire for all people.[15] Luke continues his description of the story:

> Now there were Jews living in Jerusalem, devout men from every nation under heaven. And when this sound occurred, the crowd came together, and were bewildered because each one of them was hearing them speak in his own language. They were amazed and astonished, saying, "Why, are not all these who are speaking Galileans? And how is it that we each hear them in our own language to which we were born? Parthians and Medes and Elamites, and residents of Mesopotamia, Judea and Cappadocia, Pontus and Asia, Phrygia and Pamphylia, Egypt and the districts of Libya around Cyrene, and visitors from Rome, both Jews and proselytes, Cretans and Arabs—we hear them in our own tongues speaking of the mighty deeds of God." (Acts 2:5–11)

In this account Luke stresses the racial and ethnic identity of Peter's audience: they were Jews and devout men from every nation under heaven. That is, both Jews and gentiles were together in one place. As both groups spoke in multiple languages, everyone was amazed and in disbelief and asked: How can this be? Luke identifies different ethnic groups of the gentiles in remarkable detail: Galileans, "Parthians and Medes and Elamites, and residents of Mesopotamia, Judea and Cappadocia, Pontus and Asia, Phrygia and Pamphylia, Egypt and the districts of Libya around Cyrene, and visitors from Rome, both Jews and proselytes, Cretans and Arabs" (Acts 2:7–11a). Altogether, he names fifteen regions and identifies four primary people groups. The naming of regions and people groups suggests inclusivity and extensiveness, reminiscent of the Table of Nations in Genesis 10. In fact, Luke 10:1–12 already alludes to Genesis 10; there, the sending out of the twelve disciples corresponds to the twelve tribes of Israel, and Jesus's sending out of the seventy witnesses corresponds to the seventy nations in Genesis 10.[16]

The Spirit did not discriminate between Jews and gentiles or between Cretans and Arabs: the tongues of fire were distributed among them and rested on each and every one of those present. Although the languages spoken were different, the content of the languages was unified because everyone spoke of the mighty deeds of God. Biblical scholar G. K. Beale sees Pentecost as the reversal of Babel: "God causes representatives from the same scattered nations to unite in Jerusalem in order that they might receive the blessing of understanding different languages as if all these languages were one."[17] Darrell Bock understands the speaking of God's activity in different languages as an "evangelistic enablement," so that each person can hear God's work in his or her own language.[18] Jennings perceives the Day of Pentecost as marking a beginning, much as in the book of Genesis, but without the language of beginning.

In the particular historical context of the book of Acts, "the mighty deeds of God" refers to proclaiming the death and resurrection of Jesus, and his ascension to the heavenly throne to reign as a king.[19] It is toward this end that the believers are to be witnesses of Christ, with the power of the Holy Spirit, and are to be dispersed once again from Jerusalem to all of Judea and Samaria, and even to the ends of the earth (Acts 1:8). The idea of dispersion and centralization reemerges in the new historical context. Believers, as God's representatives on the earth, are to fill the earth with a unifying purpose to share the knowledge of God and proclaim his kingdom to all flesh. This is a radical calling when one considers the historical context, in which allegiance to Caesar took precedence over all competing loyalties and the Roman Empire desired to shape the world into its own image through conquering other nations and through cultural influences, contrary to the intention of God in creation.[20]

While the incident at Pentecost converges with the story of Babel in terms of people speaking in different languages, how the two stories diverge is much more striking: At Babel, the initial unification of language was centered on human beings' endeavor to make a name for themselves and to avoid being scattered. At Pentecost, the unification appears not in the language itself but in the content of the language—people spoke of the mighty deeds of God in different languages. In this sense, Pentecost overturns Babel from a human-centered orientation to a God-centered orientation, from a form of human or imperial domination to the beginning of the reign of God.

This has profound implications for theological education. Teaching in different languages has its proper place in reaching out to the diverse demography of students from all tribes and nations. The kingdom of God is inclusive and diverse. Behind the amazement of hearing one's native tongue spoken by someone of a different race or ethnicity is the sentiment of joy and familiarity—the sentiment of "I feel like home" or the expression "we speak the same language." It also conveys the intimacy of belonging. I recall being in a church courtyard where people from different congregations were mingling and fellowshiping. There, I heard Mandarin, Cantonese, and English—the three languages that I understand and with which I identify myself. Then and there, a sense of belonging welled up in my heart. Understanding another's language brings one closer to the other.

The contents of the language spoken as well as the kind of language spoken are equally significant. The contents of theological education ought to orient one toward the knowledge of God and to God's actions in history. Speaking another person's language shows that one orients oneself toward another. It involves submission to and even love for the other's culture.[21] Through giving people the ability to speak others' languages, the Spirit is uniting them as the people of God. At Babel, people spoke different languages without understanding each other because God confused their language, whereas at Pentecost the speaking of different languages did not prevent people from understanding one another. The implication is that speaking different languages is not a curse, but lack of understanding of different languages is. On the Day of Pentecost, the Spirit privileges diversity of languages over one language, but there is unity within diversity when people speak the same content in different tongues—the same content of proclaiming the mightiness of God.

Not all those at Pentecost responded the same way. Some tried to take it all in, struggling to understand what it meant. Others sneered and dismissed the whole incident, thinking that the people who spoke in different languages were simply drunk: "And they all continued in amazement and great perplexity, saying to one another, 'What does this mean?' But others were mocking and saying, 'They are full of sweet wine'" (Acts 2:12–13). Peter took this opportunity to refute the mockers, saying that this was not a case of drunkenness but a fulfillment of what the prophet Joel prophesied long ago (Joel 2:28–32).

Joel's prophecy dealt with a locust plague that prefigured the human invasion of Israel by the Assyrians and the Babylonians as divine judgment against their sins (Joel 1–2). Joel described this future vision as the coming of the Day of Yahweh (2:1, 11). This day was characterized by meteoric "signs and wonders." It was a day of darkness and gloom, with fire and flames, a day on which the earth quaked and the heavens trembled, the sun and the moon grew dark, and the stars lost their brightness (2:2–10). Then Joel offered the promise of hope by saying that God would give Israel the early rain and the latter rain so that vegetation would sprout again (2:23–24). Yet this pouring out of physical rain is not the end of God's promise of restoration. Joel continued by prophesying that God would likewise pour out his Spirit on all people. Meteoric signs and wonders would appear again, and whoever called on the name of God would be delivered (2:28–32). The Day of Yahweh is first a day of judgment, and then a day of restoration would come through the pouring out of his Spirit on all people. By citing this passage from Joel, Peter understood and appropriated the Day of Pentecost as the beginning of the fulfillment of Joel's prophecy.

Therefore, the blessings that God intended for humanity in creating us and calling us to multiply and fill the earth are renewed in Abraham, and then in the seed of Abraham—Jesus— and then renewed again in the pouring out of the Holy Spirit. All who receive Jesus as Lord will become the seed of Abraham. All who receive the Holy Spirit will become the people of God. As a result, the identity of the people of God is no longer located in one chosen race—the Jews or the elite group in society such as the (male) priests or the (male) religious elders—but includes people of all races, ethnicities, genders, and classes. The curse of the confusion of language at Babel is averted at Pentecost, where people understand one another's language in speaking of the mighty deeds of God. Pentecostal evangelical theologian Amos Yong contends that it is not just the translatability of the gospel that is miraculous, but that "strange tongues can indeed be vehicles of the gospel and can declare the wonders of God."[22] He says the divine affirmation of many tongues also means that God embraces the many cultures of the world, since language, culture, and religion are intertwined. This invites the Asian diaspora to declare and testify in their own tongues and languages about the mighty acts of God.[23]

As we indicated earlier, Felix Liu, a Taiwanese evangelical Christian, out of his zeal for God, started a religious movement focused on church planting and evangelism that resulted in founding both a new denomination and a seminary that has been accredited by the ATS and reaches out to the Mandarin-speaking diaspora. His story is an example of the work of the Holy Spirit in our days. The Chinese language that the seminary is using in declaring the mighty acts of God testifies to the diversity and plurality of religious expression that are celebrated in the kingdom of God. The second chapter of this book shows that at Logos Seminary, women, like men, are afforded the opportunity to serve and lead in an egalitarian fashion, against the prevalent practice based on the Confucian hierarchy for women in the Asian tradition. In this sense, the Spirit replaces the old order with a new reality in the kingdom of God.

When I participate in ATS and Society of Biblical Literature meetings for ethnic minority scholars, the issue of diversity is almost always understood to equate with justice. Minority scholars perceive deep structural racism in the academy where institutions desire the color of their skin but do not offer support to guarantee their success, which is often deeply shaped by issues of race and injustice. Keri Day's book in this series reflects precisely how an obviously successful African American scholar still experiences structural racism of both the most obvious and the most subtle kinds in the academy. Willie Jennings's book in this series also illustrates the ways the faculty interview process is permeated by prejudice and bias. For historically black schools such as Howard University (or Mandarin-speaking ones like Logos), the issue of diversity also invites reflection. If the school's history and identity are oriented toward one race or ethnicity, what does "diversity" mean in these contexts? How would an institution embrace diversity but retain its cultural as well as missional identity? Though the term "diversity" is not as simple as it seems, it is certainly rooted in God's desire for humanity in general and for the academy in particular. And therefore each theological institution needs to define and affirm diversity in its own ways and also in accord with its institutional mission.

As a female Chinese theological educator, an ethnic minority in white America, a person with a diasporic identity, teaching at a diasporic institution in the United States, I am drawn more and more to the works of the Holy Spirit in my own institution as well as other institutions that desire to yield to the work of the Spirit. Although I may not identify myself as a Pentecostal evangelical Christian, I am undoubtedly compelled to embrace the vision of Pentecost for a more inclusive and diverse future in theological education.

The Heavenly Scene

However marvelous the reversal of Babel in Pentecost, it is not the apex of the story but a penultimate encounter, a prelude to what is to come. In John's eschatological vision of the throne room, he witnesses a grand worship service in which people of all nations come to worship God.

> After these things I looked, and behold, a great multitude which no one could count, from every nation and all tribes and peoples and tongues, standing before the throne and before the Lamb, clothed in white robes, and palm branches were in their hands; and they cry out with a loud voice, saying, "Salvation to our God who sits on the throne, and to the Lamb." And all the angels were standing around the throne and around the elders and the four living creatures; and they fell on their faces before the throne and worshiped God, saying, "Amen, blessing and glory and wisdom and thanksgiving and honor and power and might, be to our God forever and ever. Amen." (Rev. 7:9–12)

In this vision of the heavenly throne room, the great multitude of people is not homogeneous. There is no one dominant nation, empire, or group, but people of every nation, tribe, people group, and tongue, corresponding to all the families of the earth evoked in Genesis 12:3. The diversity expressed by this multitude is accompanied by its unity. Everyone worships the same God and shouts out their praises of adoration: "Salvation to our God who sits on the throne, and to the Lamb." In this sense, diversity is expressed and forged through unity in God and the Lamb. Alongside the multitude of people are the angelic beings, the elders of the heavenly court, and four living creatures. They all bow and worship and give blessing to God. The entire heavenly realm becomes the divine temple where God resides and reigns, and where his people worship in union. Worshiping God is the end of all things. It is also the *telos* of theological education—to bring people of all nations, tribes, and tongues (the "new Abraham") to the knowledge of God and to worship him.

The last two chapters of Revelation depict an eschatological vision of a new heaven and a new earth in which Jerusalem descends from heaven to be among humanity, just like the tabernacle of God was among his people.[24] The two realms of heaven and earth are merged into one reality: "And I saw the holy city, new Jerusalem, coming down out of heaven from God, made ready as a bride adorned for her husband. And I heard a loud voice from the throne, saying, 'Behold, the tabernacle of God is among men, and He will dwell among them, and they shall be His people, and God Himself will be among them'" (Rev. 21:2–3).

In this new reality, God dwells among human beings and the city of Jerusalem becomes the whole world. What is more, Revelation says, there will be no sea (21:1) and no temple, because God and Jesus are its temple (21:22), and no night or light of a lamp or even of the sun, because God will illumine everything: "There will no longer be any curse; and the throne of God and of the Lamb will be in it, and His bond-servants will serve Him; they will see His face, and His name will be on their foreheads. And there will no longer be any night; and they will not have need of the light of a lamp nor the light of the sun, because the Lord God will illumine them; and they will reign forever and ever" (22:3–5).

There is no curse in this eschatological vision. Since the first earth has passed away, the curse of the ground because of humanity's fall is no longer present. God has made everything new. The new humanity will become servants of God, serving him and reigning till eternity. Humanity as God's representatives on the earth in the creation of the world has found its permanent place in this final vision of the new world. The image of God has been restored and renewed in the final chapter of Scripture. The new kingdom of God will comprise people from all nations whose sole purpose is to worship God. It is in this end of the knowledge of God and the worship of God that theological education finds its meaning and purpose.

As Christianity is currently in between the birth of the church and the final eschaton at which people of all nations, tribes, and languages will worship and praise the one true God, theological education is between the times—between the pouring out of the Spirit and the glorious return of Jesus, a time when empires and their languages may seem to dominate the world, even as we look forward to a time of radical inclusivity of all languages and nations. This time is made possible by God's gift of the Spirit and expressed in our yearning for the fulfillment of salvation. The image of people at Pentecost speaking of the mighty acts of God coalesces with this eschatological vision in which everything in its diversity is unified in the worship of the one true God.

Therefore, with this end in sight, the purpose of theological education is about knowing God and participating in the missional endeavor to bring that knowledge of God to the ends of the earth so that the reign of God will be established on the earth. Realizing—making real—the reign of God is the ultimate end. Given the diverse demographics of the people of God, a plurality of languages is needed to bear witness to the reign of God on the earth. This is a good reason to offer theological education in a plurality of languages, even within one country. Mandarin-speaking seminaries, Korean-speaking seminaries, Spanish-speaking seminaries, and more are all witnesses to the beauty of the inclusivity and diversity in the kingdom of God.

Affirming Diversity in Theological Education

That the sons of Noah were dispersed all over the ancient Near East according to their families, languages, lands, and nations (Gen. 10) affirms the place of particularity in God's grand narrative: human beings, bearers of the image of God, are to rule on his behalf in order to manifest the reign of God on the earth. The people of God include those of every nation and tribe, along with their own languages and cultures in their various nuances and complexities. It is through these multiple particularities that the end of knowing and worshiping God can be accomplished.

This affirmation of particularities of language and culture has implications for theological schools. Culturally specific theological schools, along with programs designed for specific racial and ethnic groups at theological schools that try to include many groups, have important roles in the grand narrative of God's mission. If targeting a specific group of people enhances the mission or the educational effectiveness of the institution, then launching ethnically specific programs and establishing ethnically specific theological schools would contribute to the multifaceted nature of theological education and enable more people to receive it in their own languages and cultures. A monolingual context is an incomplete reflection of the kingdom of God. The lyrics of "1000 Tongues," composed by Vertical Worship Band, celebrate this linguistic plurality in the kingdom of God: "We are a sea of voices / We are an ocean of Your praise / Gathered under one name."[25]

Since language is inseparable from culture, many immigrant churches make preserving their cultural values and customs one of their primary functions. The same applies to diasporic and ethnic theological schools and programs. However, increasing educational or learning effectiveness and perpetuating language and culture through ethnic or culturally specific schools are not ends in themselves but the means to an end. Just as God's calling of Abraham is for him to become a blessing to all the families of the earth, so each diasporic or ethnic program and institution ought to serve as the medium through which a specific group of people will bless others along the way. Each particularity has to be united with the new Abraham—Jesus—and be open to the work of the Holy Spirit in these latter days. In this sense, all diasporic and ethnic theological schools or programs need to find ways to create the shelter and connection necessary for people to flourish without isolating themselves. They need to make a conscious effort to connect with the larger ecclesial body and institutions. They need to speak in their own particular languages and in languages they share with others. Both are necessary for bringing particularity and universality together. There is a place for particularity. There is also a place for shared languages that display a hope for universality. At the eschatological banquet of the Lamb, there will be people from all nations gathered to give glory to God and to the Lamb. Particularity and universality ought to be held in creative tension and harmony. As Dan Aleshire asserts, "Racial diversity is a theological virtue."[26]

Redefining Diversity at Logos Evangelical Seminary

On November 13, 2018, journalists from the In Trust Center toured several seminaries in Southern California, including Logos. One of the questions they asked the representatives of Logos was: How does diversity work at a school like Logos? I, as the acting academic dean on that day, was called to respond to this question. I said, "For Logos, diversity is not defined in terms of race and ethnicity, but in other forms of diversity. The term 'Chinese' means diversity." For a school like Logos, the issue of diversity needs to be redefined. From the macro perspective, the presence of Logos Seminary among ATS schools demonstrates ATS's commitment to diversity and Logos's contribution to racial and ethnic diversity. Likewise, the inclusion of a representative from Logos in the Theological Education between the Times project also reflects the series editor's intention to make the series diverse and inclusive.

From the micro perspective—within Logos Seminary—the understanding of diversity needs to go beyond race and ethnicity to include other strands of diversity. For example, diversity can be achieved through gender, age, generations, economic status, denominational background, physical and mental ability, and cultural contexts. Not all Chinese come from mainland China, and not all Chinese speak Mandarin with the same accents or use the same vocabulary. The Chinese diaspora is as diverse as can be—just as Hispanics/Latinos/as are not all the same. There are Hispanics from Mexico, from Spain, and from Cuba and Guatemala, for example. Although they all speak Spanish, each region has its own set of values, accents, sense of history, preferences in food, and cultural particularities. That said, since race and ethnicity are so visible in the US context, and since other forms of diversity are not as apparent as they are, the lack of diversity in race and ethnicity in an institution does create a false impression of homogeneity. In addition, the issue of diversity or lack of it is often associated with power or the domination of the majority race or ethnicity. Thus, a traditionally defined racial ethnic school or a historically black school is at a disadvantage in articulating diversity *if* diversity is defined solely by having students and faculty of many different races and ethnicities.

Since recruiting faculty with ethnicities other than Chinese who can also speak Mandarin is challenging, Logos is trying to reflect diversity in its faculty in terms of gender, age distribution, schools from which they receive their doctorates, and countries of origin. For example, of our current fourteen faculty members, seven are women and seven are men. Of these, one is white. In 2018 Logos extended a job offer to a Finnish professor who speaks Mandarin, but he declined the offer for personal reasons. Almost half of the faculty members are originally from Taiwan. Of the others, two are from mainland China, two from Hong Kong, and one has both American and Taiwanese upbringings. Many of the faculty members also lived in multiple countries before coming to Logos. In addition, most faculty members graduated from diverse institutions in the United States and the United Kingdom, and their age range also shows diversity—from the midforties to the late seventies.

At the student level, diversity at Logos encounters a different set of issues. There is enormous diversity within Chinese culture as a whole. For example, students from various provinces of China experience different cultures and dialects. Students who just came from Taiwan are different culturally from those who immigrated to the United States decades ago. Students of the 1.5 generation (those who come to the United States in their teens) are quite different culturally from first-generation Chinese, too. However, even the admittedly complex diversity that manifests among Chinese students does not trump the differences between a Chinese person and an African American person or a Chinese person and a white person or a Chinese person and a Hispanic person. Students at racially mixed theological schools have opportunities to learn from their fellow students who are of different races and ethnicities. By contrast, students at Logos are not in a context in which they can learn from fellow students who are of different races.

That said, the reality is that most graduates of Logos will serve in a Chinese ministry context rather than in a racially mixed environment. The intercultural program at Logos aims to form students to do cross-cultural missions. While Logos Seminary is not diverse in race, it reflects diversity in gender, age, generation, culture, and subculture. And these kinds of diversity might be most important for its mission.

Logos also contributes to the diversity of theological education as a wider endeavor in North America. When every school is internally diverse, the languages, cultures, practices, and traditions of minoritized groups tend to get swept away by a dominant culture. But Logos and other diasporic seminaries can preserve and renew minoritized cultures in ways that contribute to the larger diversity of the whole. The presence of all diasporic seminaries and ethnic programs bears witness to the diversity of the kingdom of God. They become indispensable pieces in the global puzzle of God's world.

In sum, Scripture affirms diversity. Diversity reflects God's desire for humanity and for his kingdom. It is indeed a theological virtue as well as a theological necessity to embrace diversity in all its manifestations. While racial and ethnic diversity is a significant issue in most theological schools, a school like Logos defines diversity beyond race and ethnicity. Logos is one piece of the whole diversity puzzle in North American theological education. Representing one among many racial ethnic groups in North America, Logos, together with the many other theological schools, participates in the realization of the kingdom of God as a diasporic entity. Therefore, in the here and now, a plurality of languages in theological education needs to be encouraged as a theological necessity. The definition of diversity and the standard for diversity in theological schools need to be redefined in terms of the institutional mission as well as by recognizing the presence of multiple layers of diversity. While the Chinese are one race but multilingual and multicultural, Americans are one language with multiple races. Both the Chinese and the Americans display homogeneity and diversity in their own ways; both ways are necessary for diversity in the deepest sense. Both understandings of diversity need to be affirmed in the kingdom of God.

In closing this chapter, I would like to borrow from Martin Luther King Jr.'s famous "I Have a Dream" speech and reframe it in the context of Logos Seminary.

I have a dream that one day Logos Seminary will be known first for its commitment to the centrality of the gospel, and not for its instructional language.

I have a dream that one day Logos Seminary will testify to the world what God is doing among the Chinese diaspora and beyond.

I have a dream that one day all the theological schools with various ecclesial traditions and cultural identities will come together to sing the glory of God in one accord.

In the next and final chapter, I will be imagining what Logos Evangelical Seminary would say to the wider communities of theological schools in North America in theological education between the times.

4

Reimagining Theological Education
for the Diaspora

As part of its continuing work to encourage diversity in its member schools, the ATS established a Committee on Race and Ethnicity (CORE). To promote its mission, twenty-two selected schools convened in Pittsburgh for a conference whose aim was to generate dialogue to promote diversity in their own institutions. The intention was that invitees would return to their respective institutions and work out a concrete plan to further the work of diversity. Representatives from schools growing out of mainline Protestant traditions, such as Harvard University, attended the conference, as did those from evangelical Protestant schools, such as Denver Seminary. Also, a few historically black seminaries such as Hood Theological Seminary and Samuel Dewitt Proctor School of Theology of Virginia Union University were represented. And then there was Logos Evangelical Seminary—the lone Chinese/Asian theological school represented at the conference; I was one of three from my school representing it at the conference.

From a bird's-eye view, among the binary groups of black and white, the presence of Logos Seminary among ATS member schools widens ATS's commitment to diversity. At the same time, Logos is not just marginal as a racial ethnic seminary but also as a seminary that does not fit into the black and white categories that organize so much of American theological education. It relates in ambiguous ways to the dominant groups in the landscape of theological schools in North America in terms of scholarship and practice. Whether the gathering is of schools aiming to serve the majority population or schools serving particular racial and ethnic groups, Logos often appears as the "other."

Another incident: When the journalists from In Trust Center visited Logos in November 2018, they asked us to "describe the cultural context of the seminary. How are teaching and learning different at Logos than at another seminary like Fuller or Gateway?" As I pondered this question, several thoughts came to mind. First, the question seems to assume that a school like Logos must have its own cultural context, different from that of a predominantly white or a multiethnic school. Second, it assumes that this cultural context renders the experience of teaching and learning different from that of other schools that are, say, predominantly white or more racially mixed. I wonder if the In Trust journalists raise the same question when they visit schools such as Fuller and Gateway, Logos's neighbors in Southern California.

As a seminary often on the "outside," Logos gets asked questions others might not. At the same time, Logos has its own distinctive questions to ask and things to say to the wider community of theological education. This chapter attempts to reimagine theological education between the times from the vantage point of Logos Seminary for the purpose of instigating hope for the future of theological education.

Commonalities We Share

Outsiders—perhaps including the In Trust representatives— often perceive a Chinese seminary as something "ethnic," "foreign," or "international." The underlying presumption is that a Chinese seminary does theological education differently than do the majority of schools in North America. The fact is: other than race and language, a school like Logos has many things in common with other theological schools. These commonalities include both the practice of theological education and the challenges that all theological schools encounter. First and foremost, Logos belongs to the broader family of evangelical schools. Traditionally, an "evangelical" has been understood as one who ascribes to the "quadrilateral of priorities," that is: Christ and the crucifixion, the authority of the Bible, the need for personal conversion, and engagement in the mission of God.[1] Seeing it from another angle, Mark Young, president of Denver Seminary, has eloquently defined what the evangelical theological position is and has named its major premises and anxieties in his book in this series. For example, evangelical theological schools uphold the gospel, emphasizing both redemption and hope. Young asserts that "Hope is the personal and communal experience of the gospel of redemption that lies at the center of evangelical theology."[2] Yet it seems that what Young had in mind was white "evangelical schools" and "evangelicals," as he shared in person at one of our TEBT meetings.

The reality is that "evangelical schools" are not limited to "white evangelicals" or schools like Dallas Theological Seminary or Talbot School of Theology. Logos Evangelical Seminary shares all the theological premises and anxieties of the evangelical faith, as the name of the school—Logos Evangelical Seminary—states explicitly. Safeguarding the evangelical faith should be the primary element that defines Logos Seminary (both to insiders and outsiders), but in racial America, this is not the case. This evangelical identity should have been acknowledged first before we delved into the educational practices in which it diverged from other theological schools.

Poet Maya Angelou has written a beautiful poem entitled "Human Family," which Apple adopted in one of its TV commercials. The poem celebrates the commonalities among all people, commonalities that inspire the reader to seek common ground rather than being divisive. After listing different types of people on the planet, Angelou ends the poem like this:

I note the obvious differences between each sort
    and type,
but we are more alike, my friends, than we are unalike.

We are more alike, my friends, than we are unalike.
We are more alike, my friends, than we are unalike.[3]

Let us reimagine the poem and identify the pronoun "We" with "Logos Evangelical Seminary." As a part of the family of theological schools in North America in general and of evangelical schools in particular, "We (Logos) are more alike, my friends, than we are unalike." For instance, as a theological school, Logos educates students for a variety of ministry and vocational options. The education at Logos involves teaching and learning. Different faculty members have different teaching styles; some are more lecture oriented, others engage students through a variety of teaching methods. Standardized course designs have been developed to make learning assessment more accurate. Like many schools, online courses and synchronized courses have also been offered extensively in recent decades. Logos is in the process of offering a fully online master of arts in Christian studies, and expects in the foreseeable future to offer more such programs. In light of the coronavirus (COVID-19) pandemic in 2020, all schools are going online to ensure a vibrant ongoing education without the geographical barrier. Like many schools, spiritual formation at Logos remains a significant aspect in the philosophy of theological education. How to form an intimate, vibrant, and ongoing relationship with God has always been at the heart of Logos's vision for theological formation. As chapter 1 indicates, the founder of the school, its first president, and professor of spiritual formation, Felix Liu, played and still plays a significant role in grounding the theological practices of students based on their spiritual formation. At the same time, Logos struggles with doing spiritual formation through online forum, as do other schools.

As is true of many schools, the curriculum at Logos Seminary includes courses on biblical studies, theological understanding, Christian practices, counseling and pastoral care, as well as missions- and ministry-related courses. Like many schools, Logos also encounters enrollment and financial challenges. Although the enrollment has generally gone up in the past, with the increase in faculty number and school facilities, it has not been keeping up with the increasing costs of operating the school. Although financially Logos has been growing steadily over the years, balancing the budget remains a constant challenge, since the majority of its income comes from individual donors. Logos also adheres to the educational standards set by ATS in all areas, including faculty development, course credits, program requirements, self-study reports for accreditation purposes, and preparation for periodic ATS site visits and focus visits. These are all examples of major commonalities that Logos shares with other theological schools. Yet, there are obvious differences too.

Differences We Hold

In chapter 2, I named seven major areas in which Logos Seminary serves as a counternarrative to the dominant narratives in theological education. In this section, I name a few more examples that further illustrate the distinctiveness of the seminary.

Learning

In student learning, the major difference between Logos Seminary and other seminaries like Fuller and Gateway is language. As I have mentioned frequently, the primary instructional language at Logos is Mandarin, except for the Asian American Ministry course, which is conducted in English. The content of the instruction, however, is quite similar; only the language used in teaching and learning is different from that of other seminaries in North America.

Another distinction is that learning is a holistic formational process. It is not merely knowledge-based learning in the classrooms or learning done through reading assignments and homework. The education at Logos is holistic and includes spiritual formation, academic excellence, ministerial competencies, and Christian living. Learning also takes place through community building and through working with other students. Thus, Logos students are required to go to chapel, participate in worship practice, and lead weekly prayer meetings at school and daily prayer meetings in their dorms. Every semester, each faculty member is assigned a small group of five or more students among whom to cultivate relationships as well as offer guidance, support, and encouragement as the students build community among themselves. Through this small-group experience, students learn how to share their lives, voice their concerns, and find a space to be honest with one another. Many friendships are built through this small-group experience.

Many years ago, I had a small group of five male students and a few female students. The five male students were all single at the time. At one of our meetings, we prayed for each of their future marriages. A few years later, all of them graduated from Logos and four out of five, one after another, got married and have been serving God in different churches in the United States and in Taiwan ever since. I attended their weddings with great joy. Now, some of them have children of their own. As we look back, we can see that those prayers we offered in our small group were being answered. Bonds among these five guys were being forged through their common quest for a wife and a family with whom to serve God. Another student in my small group graduated and relocated to Ohio. He served at a local Chinese church there. When he was about to be ordained at his church, he asked me to make a video recording my congratulatory words of blessing to him, a video he then showed during his ordination service. The bond between teacher and student often lasts far beyond graduation. At Logos, a significant aspect of learning about Christian faith, relationship, and community takes place in small groups.

Yet for all such successes, we also have some struggles. For example, cultivating intercultural and cross-cultural competency has been difficult at Logos Seminary, owing to its lack of a racially diverse student body. The "holistic" formational process is defined in the Chinese context rather than the Western context.

Teaching

Although the content of our teaching at Logos is similar to that at other theological schools, particularly other evangelical schools, yet, in addition to the instructional language, teaching at Logos also involves application in the context of immigrant churches and in the Chinese diaspora. Since the majority of Logos students will serve in Chinese churches, whether in North America or elsewhere, the appropriation of the knowledge learned is contextual. In this sense, faculty members often use Chinese churches as the fertile ground in which to apply biblical knowledge and ministerial skills. For example, when teaching the book of Daniel, I ask students to describe the similarities and differences between an immigrant culture and a native culture, and the struggles and challenges Daniel encountered in his deportation to Babylon. I also ask students to reflect on the temporary nature of earthly empires and the lack of religious freedom in China. Those faculty members who have been pastoring Chinese churches in North America encourage students to connect the struggles of the Corinthian church with those that Chinese churches face today.

Instructors of Asian American Ministry introduce students to the history of Asian Americans in North America, their plight as both "model minority" and "perpetual foreigner," their identity formation and struggles as well as the racism and prejudice they suffer as Asian Americans. The children of many Logos students were born or raised in the United States. With that in mind, the Asian American Ministry course advances awareness of second-generation English ministry and how they can better serve at an immigrant church, which often involves ministry to their English-speaking generation. As for those students who will serve in Asia upon graduation, this Asian American Ministry course broadens their cultural understanding and forces them to rethink ministry in a variety of cultural contexts. That said, not many students at Logos feel comfortable speaking in English. Owing to the high Chinese population in the greater Los Angeles area, English proficiency is not necessary for survival, which does not help the students to acculturate or feel the necessity of assimilating to the larger English-speaking American culture. Increasing English proficiency has long been a struggle for Logos Seminary and will be so for the foreseeable future. This is one of the areas with which Logos needs to grapple in order to form in students greater intercultural competence and to minister to a wider audience, particularly to the next generations of American-born or American-raised Chinese.

Immigrant and Diasporic Identity

Another question that the journalists from the In Trust Center raised during their visit in November 2018 was this: "Do students who are themselves also immigrants learn or form community in ways that are different from those students who were born in the United States?" This question reflects a major distinction of the student population at Logos Seminary. As a diasporic seminary, all students are either first-generation immigrants or visa students. Even those who immigrated to the United States two, three, or more decades ago remain immigrants who have not assimilated to the mainstream American culture and do not plan to do so. The immigrant identity is at the core of their being. Most of them will form friendships with fellow immigrants and form immigrant communities at Chinese churches, serving other Chinese immigrants in the Chinese diaspora.

At Logos, there are no American-born Chinese (ABC) or second-generation Asian American students. In the past, Logos has had a limited number of 1.5 generation students. These are students who immigrated to the United States when they were teenagers and who are fluent in both English and Mandarin (although some of them claim they are good at neither language). This unique demographic of the Logos student body renders it both an immigrant community where America is the host country and the idea of "home" is ambivalent, and an international school, with many students coming from outside the United States, some of whom return to their countries of origin upon graduation. For such students, home is their country of origin and not the United States. In reality, Logos is a diasporic community that acknowledges people from all global migrations that flow through and help create it.

In this immigrant and diasporic context, students are keenly aware of their pilgrim status living in America. They feel that their permanent home awaits in heaven. The pilgrim identity is one of the reasons that compel many young students in their early twenties to choose to invest their lives in ministry. Much as the history of Israel arises in the context of a suzerain-vassal relationship to major empires of the world such as Egypt, Babylon, Persia, Greece, and Rome, so too those students who are themselves immigrants or international students resonate more easily with the plight of the Israelites and border-crossing biblical characters such as Joseph, Moses, Ruth, Daniel, and Esther than do those students who were born in empires such as the United States. In this sense, having an immigrant identity is an asset rather than a liability, because it helps one to understand better the place of the marginalized as well as seeing the Christian journey from a pilgrim perspective awaiting the eternal home in heaven. Additionally, those with an immigrant or diasporic identity often engage more effectively in intercultural ministry contexts than do those who have been exposed to only one dominant culture.

Given the increasing number of racial ethnic, minority, and international students in theological schools in North America, theological educators need not only to be aware of their immigrant or diasporic identity but also to regard it as an asset. This identity should be valued rather than dismissed or belittled. Racial ethnic and minority students experience and live in more than one world in their lives. They perceive the dominant culture differently. Their own experience as a racial ethnic minority in the United States also means that they have something to offer in the global dialogues on theology, culture, ethics, and more. Their perspective can enrich the perspectives of the dominant narratives. The presence of racial ethnic and minority students makes the classroom and the school more like the eschatological banquet of the Lamb. Their presence is to be valued and appreciated. Their voices and viewpoints are to be taken seriously. Both the dominant groups and the minoritized groups have something valuable to offer to each other and to all those at the banquet.

Many scholars and theologians of color were educated in seminaries in North America. They write from their place as ethnic minorities, but they also engage in global theology. Scholars such as Justo González, Fernando Segovia, Keri Day, Elizabeth Conde-Frazier, Hosffman Ospino, Willie Jennings, and Amos Yong are notable examples. It is important for faculty to provide a broad theological and cultural platform in the classroom, so that the minds of the students from various races and cultures are widened and enlarged to imagine a new future. Who knows? Because of our teaching, one or more of the students from our classrooms might become the next Justo González, Fernando Segovia, Keri Day, Elizabeth Conde-Frazier, Hosffman Ospino, Willie Jennings, or Amos Yong! To create a global theological and cultural spectrum for the students, faculty need to learn to think globally and to practice accordingly. Our future depends on it. A mind that is able to go beyond one's own cultural and theological limitations does not happen overnight; it needs to be cultivated and expanded.

Religious Freedom

There is broad freedom of speech and religion in the United States. Formally sanctioned prayers by school authorities or teachers are banned and overt evangelistic activities are prohibited in public schools in the United States, but these limits are actually in the *service* of religious freedom for all, with the goal that no one religion should be dominant on the public school campus. People can go to church without worrying about getting arrested. People can express their faith freely without worrying that they might end up in jail. This is not the case in countries such as China, where public assembly for any religious purpose, let alone holding an evangelistic meeting or sharing the gospel with someone in a public arena, is considered illegal. Since 2018, China has tightened its policy regulating religious practice. Any public remarks that advocate for Christianity or writings that discuss Christianity are grounds for arrest. Some churches have been torn down by the government. Others have been forced to close or relocate because of frequent warnings by local officials. Crosses—the symbol of Christianity—are taken down by order of the government. Pastors and church leaders are arrested for either illegal gathering or preaching the Bible. In a country where there is lack of religious freedom, Christians live in a state of suffering and persecution. They are not able to pray or sing Christian songs out loud, nor are they able to profess their faith freely to others for fear that they will end up in prison.

Imagine students who come from that context to the United States to receive theological education. They constantly have decisions to make: Should they use their real names? How much information can they reveal about themselves? Who is watching them? What will happen to their family members back home if they "get caught" here in the States? Should they return to China upon graduation, knowing that they cannot participate in ministry openly? Should they apply for religious asylum here in the United States, and who from back home would be willing to provide evidence for their religious practice if they do apply for religious asylum? Wouldn't it get them in trouble? These are some of the questions and dilemmas that students from China encounter while staying in North America, questions and dilemmas that may sound "foreign" to those who have enjoyed religious freedom of expression their whole lives. Likewise, students who come from Muslim countries but have converted to Christianity in the United States may face similar challenges.

Living in the larger context of religious persecution, students therefore resonate with the experience of the early churches, which were under persecution until the time of Constantine, who made Christianity the official religion of the empire in the fourth century CE. Human flourishing, which is at the heart of Christianity in the West, does not ring true to the lived experience of these students. Rather, suffering and persecution, which become the true marks of Christianity, define what Christianity is all about. Students from countries that do not have religious freedom understand Christianity entirely differently than do those who have always enjoyed it. So do those who come from war-torn countries such as Syria and Ukraine or any country that does not ensure religious freedom.

At the root of religious freedom is the issue of human rights. One student from China told me that one major difference she noticed in America is that people sing praises loudly in worship services, which she could not imagine ever happening in China. She also said that when she was in China, every prayer she and her church members prayed ended in tears. Upon graduation, some of these students from China choose to stay in the United States, pastoring Chinese churches. Others return to China, pastoring house churches, knowing they will likely have to remain "underground" or face arrest if caught engaging in Christian activities. Some may judge those who choose to stay in the United States rather than return to China as "choosing the easy path" or "betraying" their own country. Yet the reality is that as the number of immigrants from China and the number of immigrant churches continue to soar, pastors with a Chinese background are also needed here in the United States to minister to the new waves of Chinese immigrants. The phenomenon of dispersion at Babel and in the early churches resurfaces in contemporary America, where Christianity continues to be propagated through the Chinese diaspora.

In 2019, Hong Kong experienced tremendous chaos touched

off by the question of whether Hongkongers accused of crimes should be extradited to China for trial and sentencing. Citizens of Hong Kong, the government of Hong Kong, as well as church communities are divided about the issue. Some support the Chinese government while others are against it. News reports feature police brutality and people's protests, along with clips of tear gas being fired at civilians by the Hong Kong police. The people of Hong Kong are in turmoil. Streets are full of umbrellas (a symbol of the protests) and trash from the confrontations between the police and the people. Infrastructure is paralyzed because of the workers' strikes and protests. Who would have thought that this could happen in contemporary Hong Kong? What will be the future of Hong Kong? Will it be able to enjoy religious freedom in the future if China continues to exert authority over it? In light of this newly contested reality of political and religious freedom, the existence of a diasporic seminary like Logos provides a safe space for students from China or Hong Kong to learn and study theology in their own language without any intervention or repression from authorities in their countries of origin. In the United States, whose Constitution is founded on the freedom of speech and religious liberty for all, the human mind can indeed be free to think, meditate, and reflect on the God who is not confined by any earthly authorities. In diasporic seminaries such as Logos, students from countries facing repression of religion are able to use the vast and rich theological resources to create a new future for themselves and for the later generations in the diaspora and beyond.

Even with this distinctive mission, Logos Evangelical Seminary remains similar to other theological schools in its general educational practices and challenges. It shares its evangelical faith and anxieties with other evangelical schools, both those that are predominantly white and those that are multiracial or identified with another minoritized group. At the same time, Logos is distinctive in the areas of learning, teaching, immigrant and diasporic identity, as well as in the mission of providing a safe haven of religious freedom for Mandarin speakers. These distinctive features enable a school like Logos to identify more easily with the predicament of the early churches and the essence of Christianity as a suffering body. That identification with Christ's suffering body makes possible a witness that could be of value for the wider Christian community. There is a place for a school like Logos in theological education between the times.

What Would Logos Say to the Theological Schools in North America?

What does Logos have to say to North American theological schools in this time between the times to further a hopeful future for theological education? Below, building on what I have said so far in this book, I suggest seven conversation points.

Logos Recognizes the Work of the Holy Spirit among the Diaspora

While generally speaking, Christianity is declining in the West, it is flourishing and growing elsewhere, such as in the Chinese and Hispanic diasporas. The presence of Chinese seminaries in North America reflects the emergence of Chinese Christians and the need for theological education in the Chinese language to minister to the Chinese diaspora. Diaspora after Babel serves its redemptive purpose of leading people to Christ and declaring the mighty work of God. Felix Liu always taught his students to yield to the Holy Spirit. If the Holy Spirit is working among the Chinese diaspora, should not other theological schools pay attention to the Spirit's movement and whereabouts? While the work of the Holy Spirit among the Chinese diaspora may not appear to have a direct bearing on the elite schools or other minoritized schools in North America, knowing what, how, and where the Holy Spirit works would expand and shape their understanding of pneumatology as well as eschatology.

The increasing presence of diasporic theological schools and members of minoritized racial and ethnic groups in other theological schools is a microcosm of the gradual process of the realization of the kingdom of God here on the earth. In contemporary America, the Spirit is at work in plain sight among the Chinese diaspora. This has implications for faculty hiring and educating students with diasporic identities. Hiring a faculty of diverse racial and cultural background is not just the right thing to do politically, but, more importantly, it is the right thing to do biblically and theologically. Theological schools need to prepare for a future in which intercultural competence and a kingdom perspective of theological education are absolutely critical to form students in doing the kingdom work in the increasing pluralistic world.

Logos Represents a Third Voice in Theological Education

The thriving of Logos Seminary and other Chinese seminaries in North America sends a message to the world of theological education that diasporic theological schools and ethnic programs have a place under the sun. Theological schools with a strong presence of minoritized and international students need to adjust to this reality. In light of the "invasion" of racial ethnic minorities in predominantly white schools, Willie Jennings notes the intricate dynamic between scholars of color and white scholars. Jennings names three areas that need to change in that dynamic: (1) academic theological conversation; (2) the teaching life in the theological academy; and (3) the formation process of students.[4] Regarding Jennings's first point, there are two groups of scholars. One group prioritizes their own discipline or subject matter over racial identity. The other group prefers to "imagine their subject matter enclosed within its own internal logics and order of knowing that are only comprised by identity matters."[5] Both groups are aware of the other's presence, but they rarely engage in shared intellectual exploration.

According to Jennings, another area that needs to change is teaching life. He observes that many predominantly white theological institutions center on the white male as "the abiding image of education being done well," and notes how this affects the racial ethnic faculty in scholarship, teaching, and curricular vision.[6] In addition, the students of color have difficulty mapping the complexities of life in this racially mixed reality when they are coerced into assimilating to the white norm, and thus their process of theological formation is hindered. Likewise, the lack of intellectual collaboration between white students and students of color stunts the growth of both groups.[7] While Jennings insightfully spells out the dynamic between both student groups in the ecology of theological schools, there is a third narrative of which theological educators need to be aware—the emergence of diasporic schools.

Knowledge, particularly theological knowledge, is limited when seen from the vantage point of only one or two dominant groups of people. While racial injustice is a serious matter, so are other forms of injustice, such as the lack of global perspectives and inclusivity in constructing theology. The emergence of diasporic schools, though it may not significantly change the dynamics between the binary white and black groups at the present time, adds a third voice to the existing groups, which alters the current conversations on race, ethnicity, theology, and culture. This third voice embodies a pluralistic, global, and missional and kingdom perspective in the present conversation. Including the third voice will indeed be "the change we need" for the future of theological education.

Logos Wrestles with the Future of the MDiv Degree

In the past, the MDiv degree was perceived as the professional degree through which future ministers and pastors become trained to be paid clergy. In recent years, however, many theological schools have cut the total credit of the MDiv program from more than ninety units to around seventy units. Some schools are contemplating whether to follow this trend while others are resisting it. This reduction of credit units shortens the length of time needed to complete the degree. It also means that students graduate with less debt. From a practical perspective, all this is good news for students. However, most theological schools, when faced with reducing the credit hours of the MDiv degree, cut biblical language courses. Some schools turn Hebrew and Greek courses into what are called "tool courses," in which students learn how to use the digital and electronic software to exegete the biblical text rather than learning the languages in the traditional way, by memorizing vocabulary, parsing verbs, and diagramming syntax. While learning how to use the language tools is important, this seems to be a "quick fix" and a "shortcut" to more foundational learning that is based on mastering the languages so that one can be a better interpreter of Scripture.

The status of the MDiv as a professional degree is changing. In the West, many students choose it as a path to discern God's call and not as an opportunity to receive seminary education after they have ascertained God's call to pastoral ministry. Students may certainly complete the shorter MDiv program sooner and with less debt—but at the expense of their competence in Hebrew and Greek. If future pastors are incompetent in using the original biblical languages to illuminate the significance of Scripture, how might that affect the culture of the church, the quality of preaching, and the depth of teaching and learning of the pastors and the congregations? While I agree that one does not need to master Hebrew and Greek to become a good, faithful, and effective pastor, the enduring quality of the biblical languages in shaping our understanding of the biblical text may be more profound than our eyes can see. The wisdom and the insight that come from grounding one's teaching and preaching on a solid biblical and theological foundation simply cannot be replaced by a shortcut course on biblical languages. If the purpose of the MDiv is to produce effective leaders, then the leadership model would seem to be sufficient. However, if its purpose includes producing people who are also good *preachers*, then retaining the biblical languages in the curriculum seems necessary.

As of the 2019–2020 academic year, the MDiv program at Logos still has ninety-two credit hours, including twenty-four required credits for the Bible courses (three required Old Testament courses and two required New Testament courses) and nine required credits for Hebrew and Greek. The understanding of the MDiv degree as forming and equipping future pastors endures at Logos. The understanding of the meaning and function of "pastors," however, is changing. In the Chinese context, shepherding the congregation outweighs everything. That shepherding in many cases implies caring and preaching to feed the soul and the mind of the congregation. As a professor of Hebrew and the Old Testament, I know I am biased on this issue of reducing biblical language courses for the MDiv degree or from other biblical degree programs. It would be a great loss if future pastors did not have the opportunity to learn Scripture in its original languages. This issue will persist into the near future. Logos Seminary is not unique in its approach, as other schools such as Dallas Theological Seminary also place great significance on developing students' competency in biblical languages. I hope that more schools will see the significance of biblical languages in shaping future pastors and how it relates directly to the ecology of the church.

In a time of global migration and diaspora, Christianity is spreading far and wide through immigrant churches. The sacredness of the MDiv degree as a path to pastoral ministry deserves to be maintained. The necessity of keeping Hebrew and Greek in the MDiv curriculum also deserves to be considered seriously. My wish is that pastors who receive the MDiv will be able to handle the Word of God accurately with insights gained from the biblical languages so that the quality and the depth of preaching and teaching in God's global church will continue to be strong into the future. This is not to say that solid preaching alone is adequate for leading a congregation toward fulfilling God's purposes, but it is nevertheless an essential part of being a pastor, a shepherd through teaching Scripture. Given the significance of the biblical languages for preaching, there may still be something to the professional model of theological education's insistence on putting knowledge to use. Logos shows how that

model needs to endure as long as there are preachers in need
of education.

Logos Encourages the Communal Responsibility of Ensuring
Debt-Free Theological Education

Compared to students at other schools, students at Logos Seminary incur minimal educational debt. This is due to a combi-
nation of factors unique to the context of Logos and the larger
Chinese culture. The support that religious communities show to
seminary students and the reality of visa students whose financial
stability (or ability to pay) is a prerequisite for enrollment are part
of the reason. At a time when theological schools in North America are constantly bombarded with financial crises, budget cuts,
relocation, and downsizing, encouraging a debt-free education
achieved through communal support seems to be a way to move
forward. How to do it depends on how the school articulates the
necessity and benefits of a debt-free education through a communal effort. In the context of Chinese Christian culture, necessary finances for a theological education are always a communal
responsibility. When a person goes to seminary (especially for an
MDiv degree), it is not just an individual matter, but a matter of
the whole church. Given this cultural and theological mind-set,
financial support of the student's theological education becomes
the church's spiritual offering to God and an investment in the
kingdom of God. This goes contrary to the individualization in
the West, where seminary students are typically on their own
financially and tend to graduate with significant debt. When it
comes to theological education, there is a place for individuality,
autonomy, and self-assertion, but there should also be room for
communal support, mutuality, and interdependence.

A seminary professor from another seminary once told me
that each student represents a future church. The number of
graduates reflects the number of churches that will exist to fulfill
the Great Commission. Perhaps this communal way of perceiving theological education will persuade the West to consider a

more sustainable future in theological education. Seminary students intending to do God's work should not struggle financially. Going to seminary is not merely an individual decision, but a kingdom matter, an effort that deserves to be honored and supported financially by family members as well as by ecclesial and denominational communities.

Logos Creates an Openness for Plurality of Languages in Theological Education

Theological schools in North America use predominantly one language among the many races of students enrolled, whereas in Chinese theological schools like Logos students are of one race but represent multiple cultures and languages. In the larger landscape of theological education in the United States, the prevalence and prestige of using English in speaking, reading, and writing dominate. Students measure their academic competence by how well they communicate in English. Those who speak English as a second language are compelled to fit into mainstream theological schools by imitating the American accents and verbal as well as written expressions. English becomes the standard and norm by which assimilation takes place, and immigrant scholars or ethnic minoritized groups are marginalized based on their English proficiency. Just as scholars of color advocate for decolonizing the Bible through exposing its cultural and gender bias, so too theological education needs to decolonize the language of instruction by exposing its cultural and linguistic bias. Since Babel, a plurality of languages has defined the ecology of human beings. If a plurality of languages was a negative matter, God would have eradicated it at Pentecost. Instead, Pentecost reaffirms the beauty of the plurality of languages and thus reaffirms the place of culture in understanding God and his work on the earth.

Theological schools must learn to accept the fact that no one language represents all and no single language can capture the complexity and multiplicity of the human intellect and human cultures. For example, while the English name of Logos means

"Word" in Greek, its Chinese translation, "Dao," includes the meanings of both Word and Way. As such, it carries the image of a path—the right path to God—which would definitely be lost in translation. Therefore, faculty publications in all languages should be celebrated, not just those published in English. When faculty members publish in languages other than English, their publications contribute to global Christianity as well as to the mission of God, which, after all, involves people of all nations and languages. It contributes to academic and cultural diversity. Students for whom English is a second language need to be valued for who they are and for their versatility in language and culture. Students of color are not "secondary citizens" to those who speak perfect American English. At the eschatological table of God, people from all tribes and nations will speak in their own languages and sit together as God's people. Sponsoring programs conducted in different languages—whether in Chinese, Korean, or Spanish—would be a way for schools to participate in the kingdom of God and to show that all languages are means by which to know God and to glorify God.

Logos Cultivates the Formation of Communal Identity in a Digital Age

Chinese culture, like many Asian cultures, Jewish culture, and Hispanic culture, is family and community oriented. This is in contrast to Western culture, which prizes independence and individuality. Learning and formation take place not just in the individual sphere but also through community. Therefore, theological schools would do well to consider incorporating community as a vehicle of student learning and formation. This has to be done intentionally with specific emphasis on building relationships among students. Since ministry is about people, learning in the context of community would help students to develop relational competency so as to serve more capably in ministry contexts upon graduation.

In his book on leadership, Fuller Theological Seminary

professor Tod Bolsinger writes that a transformational leadership model lies at the overlapping intersection of three leadership components: technical competence, adaptive capacity, and relational congruence.[8] While seminaries may effectively form students in technical competence, such as in biblical studies and preaching, the areas of adaptive capacity and relational congruence may be more challenging. Cultivating a communal context where students can learn both on their own and by working with and relating to others will be a necessity for the future of theological education, since ministry is largely about people and how to lead them toward fulfilling God's purposes.

Spiritual formation and character formation seem to take on a different form in an online platform. Students are formed spiritually not by a face-to-face interaction with one another but through a screen. While I do not deny the effectiveness of interactions through a screen, it is not the same as a whole-bodied, face-to-face encounter. The Theological Education between the Times project has been done in a communal context. For two years, members met three times a year in different cities of the United States while we worshiped, prayed, shared, discussed, and fellowshiped as a community. The relationships among the members could not have been forged the same way if we had met one another only in an online setting. The online platform has its merits and limits—as we are finding out at Logos Seminary. But we have discovered that the spiritual formation course is best done through face-to-face interactions on the main California campus or on our Chicago campus. Given the prevalence of fully online seminary degree programs elsewhere, compounded with the threat of pandemic like COVID-19 in 2020, it may be only a matter of time before Logos joins this trend. Yet tension remains, as leadership and faculty struggle to contemplate the impact of a formation process that is achieved through interactions via electronic screens.

Logos Modifies Educational Tools in Teaching Diasporic and Minority Students

The racism or prejudice experienced by many racial ethnic minority students and international students, especially when they live in the dominant culture, manifests itself in different ways. Some students express their anger about injustice outwardly through direct verbal confrontation with the dominant group or with the perceived authority. Others suppress their feelings and remain silent in public. Students for whom English is not their native language may feel uncomfortable speaking up in public settings and are silent to avoid being ridiculed or looked down upon. American culture places great emphasis on how one speaks English and uses that as a marker to gauge one's intelligence and competence. By this measure, a person whose spoken English is not perceived as American (or even more pointedly, not as a particular kind of American) is often considered less competent. In fact, those who speak English "with an accent" typically are simply persons who speak more than one language—hardly an attribute to be mocked. They are at least bilingual and are familiar with two or more cultures.

In addition, American culture places great importance on how vocal one is in a group setting. Being vocal means someone has a voice. He or she has something to contribute to the group. Those who are silent are considered invisible and irrelevant to advancing the group agenda or discussion. This is particularly true in online classes and online meetings. In addition, the honor and shame culture inherited by many Asians also means that public speaking is a way to boost how one is perceived and regarded if one speaks English well, or to incur shame if one speaks English haltingly or with an accent that is not appreciated. To avoid the prospect of incurring shame (upon oneself or one's ethnic community), some students remain silent.

In light of these cultural factors, below I offer a few pedagogical suggestions for theological educators in teaching racial ethnic, minority, and international students in the classroom.

Reduce "Popcorn-Style" Group Dialogue   In this common Western pedagogical method, an instructor opens up discussion to a group of people or to the whole classroom. Anyone who wants to speak can, and those who prefer not to don't have to. This way of teaching has its merits. Instructors consider it civil and respectful, and it saves anyone from being singled out or embarrassed. The right to speak relies solely on the individuals' free will. However, for those who do not speak English as their primary language, or who have suffered for being a minority student, or who are simply timid, popcorn-style discussion can be a recipe for disaster. It works only when all participants feel comfortable speaking up in such settings and in very small groups. Groups larger than four or five people tend to make popcorn-style discussion ineffective for racial ethnic and minoritized students because it is too threatening and stressful. It creates an opportunity to suffer shame, and shame is an unbearable feeling that most people try by all means to avoid.

Use a Variety of Communication Models   We have already established that Western culture places particular emphasis on speaking. It is the principal form of communication by which one's intelligence and competence are judged. This puts most racial ethnic and minority students for whom English is not their primary or dominant language at a significant disadvantage. However, instructors can engage racial ethnic and minority students in the learning process by asking all students to write down their questions or put their thoughts in writing first, or even asking students to use pictures, drawings, images, or music to describe their thoughts. Using a variety of communication tools enhances student learning, not just in the face-to-face classroom situations but also in online courses. Communication is not achieved only verbally; writing, listening, drawing, texting, gaming, and playing can all be part of the learning process.

Assign Specific Duties and Tasks for Empowerment   Racial ethnic and minority students who feel powerless in a classroom in the presence of the dominant group can be empowered if the instructor assigns them specific duties and tasks. For example, the instructor can designate them facilitators in a small-group discussion—not to single them out but to maintain a balance of students in each group.

I have found that these pedagogical practices create greater equality in the balance and perception of power. They can help all students, both in the dominant group and in minoritized groups, to develop intercultural competence along the way.

Conclusion

In theological education between the times, engaging a global perspective on teaching and learning is a necessity and not merely a choice. With the emergence of diasporic schools and ethnic programs, and the increasing number of racial ethnic, international, and minoritized students, theological educators are facing a new future that is unlike the past. In this chapter, I have highlighted the commonalities that Logos Evangelical Seminary shares with other theological schools, as well as ways in which it differs from them. I have also proposed seven conversation points that the experience of a school like Logos can offer to the wider theological world. I hope that ongoing dialogue among theological schools will forge an understanding between dominant groups and minoritized groups in the practices of theological education, so that together we may face the diverse future of theological education with enthusiasm, confidence, and joy.

In theological education between the times, change happens rapidly. Over the course of the two years in which I was engaged in writing this book, more and more theological schools have experienced leadership turnovers, campus relocations, and on-line course innovations. These are some of the means schools use to address the financial, societal, and religious changes in theological schools. What we are facing today is unlike what we have faced at any other time in the history of theological education. This has been especially true since the start of the COVID-19 pandemic. It is a critical time in which to converse about our challenges, to strategize about how to tackle the changing landscape in theological education, and to move forward with hope.

Conclusion

The Theological School as an Estuary

In this book, I have shared a story from the vantage point of Logos Evangelical Seminary, a Chinese seminary in the United States where the major historical narratives in North America intersect with a new wave of diasporic seminaries. I attempted to reenvision the future of theological education in a way that embraces both particularity and universality. In 2019, Logos celebrated its thirtieth anniversary and recast its vision and revised its mission statement in order to meet the future. It is not alone in doing so. All theological schools are adjusting to meet the various changes in theological education. As the number of diasporic seminaries and ethnic programs increases, new ways of thinking and doing theological education among all theological schools are necessary to welcome the future. This book is only one in a series of books that explore theological education between the times. As we all continue to read and reflect on theological education from various angles, viewpoints, and social locations, a sketch of the larger picture is bound to emerge. Along with it will come a need for further dialogue and reimagining the future of theological education.

I would like to end this book with an image of an estuary. An estuary is a tidal mouth of a large river, where the ocean's salty tide meets the freshwater stream. It is a space with a partly enclosed coastal body of water with one or more rivers or streams flowing into it. At the same time, it is also a space connected to the open sea. Therefore, an estuary is a transitional area between riverine and maritime environments, and so it is subject to both influences. On the one hand, there is the influx of salty seawater, and on the other hand, there is the influx of freshwater. As a result, the estuary provides a high level of nutrients and becomes the most fertile natural habitat in the world for marine creatures. As a diasporic seminary in the United States, Logos is an estuary where students from different parts of the world come together to learn, to know God, and to be formed into missional servants. The fluidity between the cultural and sociological identity of the students makes the school a vibrant Christian community because it is not stagnant. The water currents are always flowing from different directions. Whether they are converging, diverging, or fusing together, there is always something new emerging in such a faith community.

People who remain or stay temporarily in the tidal mouth of an estuary realize their transient state, that this place is not their permanent home and that there are larger purposes out there as they flow out from this space into other parts of the world. What they absorbed in the estuary they are to take along to bless others. Theological education between the times is like such an estuary where old and new tides collide and connect in order to create something new. May these new things that emerge from the flowing of multiple streams bear witness to the continuing work of God in theological schools in the diaspora so that together we will sing God's glory among the nations! To that end, we move forward with joy and hope.

For Further Thought

1. Should a diasporic school like Logos continue to use Mandarin as its instructional language in the future, or should it consider offering bilingual tracks in order to form students in intercultural competency? Why or why not?

2. At a diasporic school, there is a tension between reinforcing a particular ethnic or cultural identity and embracing a global perspective of the kingdom of God. How do we go about striking a balance between the two? What are some specific ways we can do theological education that honors both ethnic particularity and the universality of the gospel?

3. What are some gains and losses of a theological school that lacks racial and ethnic diversity? How might that lack affect the culture of the church in the future?

Notes

Introduction

1. Julius-Kei Kato, *Religious Language and Asian American Hybridity* (New York: Palgrave Macmillan, 2016), preface.

2. Ted A. Smith, "Model M and Its Afterlives," Currie Lecture, Austin Presbyterian Theological Seminary, January 31, 2017, https://austinseminarydigital.org/items/show/1159.

Chapter 1

1. The following story is based on interviews with Felix Liu on August 30, 2017, and March 7, 2018. The seminary archive is published in Andrew Su, ed., *Logos, Marching Forward! Celebrating Logos' 20th Anniversary, 1989–2009* (Taipei, Taiwan: Grace Publishing House, 2009).

2. Unless otherwise indicated, all Scriptures are taken from the New American Standard Bible.

3. The School of World Mission has since been renamed the School of Intercultural Studies, and has also been reorganized again, with the same dean serving both the School of Intercultural Studies and the School of Theology.

4. From here until the end of the chapter, I consulted the anonymous publication *Evangelical Formosan Church: 40th Anniversary Commemorative Volume* (Los Angeles: EFCGA, 2010), 23–24, and have drawn on materials from an interview with Felix Liu of April 26, 2017.

5. Iris Chang, *The Chinese in America: A Narrative History* (New York: Penguin Books, 2003), 283.

6. The organization was founded in 1976. Its mission is to unite Chinese churches to proclaim the gospel until the return of Christ. Its website is http://www.cccowe.org/.

7. As quoted in the *Baptist Herald and Friend of Africa* (October 1842) and "The Missionary Herald," *Baptist Magazine* 35 (January 1843): 41.

8. Felix Fu-Li Liu, "The Relationship between Forgiveness and Christian Wholistic Healing in Biblical Study and Pastoral Ministry" (PhD diss., Fuller Theological Seminary, 2000). The dissertation is unpublished in English but has been published in Chinese as *O Lord, I Want to Be Healed*, trans. Dora Chien (Hong Kong: Tien Dao Publishing House, 2011). In his original dissertation, Liu spelled the word "wholistic" instead of "holistic." For clarity's sake, I will use "holistic" in quotations from the document in this chapter. Hereafter, page references to this work will be placed in parentheses in the text.

9. My translation is from the original Chinese in Liu, *O Lord, I Want to Be Healed*, 21.

10. En Jen Cheng, quoted in *Evangelical Formosan Church*, 39.

11. Jay Kuo, "Vision of EFC 2020 Jubilee," in *Evangelical Formosan Church*, 12.

12. Su, *Logos, Marching Forward!*, 179.

13. The founding of the Logos Taiwan campus was aided by Logos Los Angeles. Technically speaking, since Logos Taiwan has its own board and administrative system, it is not considered a branch campus of Logos–Los Angeles but a sister campus.

14. M. Daniel Carroll R., *Christians at the Border: Immigration, the Church, and the Bible* (Grand Rapids: Brazos, 2008), 1–42.

15. Carroll R., *Christians at the Border*, 34–35.

16. Carroll R., *Christians at the Border*, 38.

17. Carroll R., *Christians at the Border*, 40.

18. Daniel O. Aleshire, *Earthen Vessels: Hopeful Reflections on the Work and Future of Theological Schools* (Grand Rapids: Eerdmans, 2008), 129.

19. Aleshire, *Earthen Vessels*, 129.

20. *Aleshire, Earthen Vessels*, 130.

21. Lois McKinney Douglas, "Globalizing Theology and Theological Education," in *Globalizing Theology: Belief and Practice in an Era of World Christianity*, ed. Craig Ott and Harold A. Netland (Grand Rapids: Baker Academic, 2006), 274.

22. James Lane, "The 10 Most Spoken Languages in the World," *Babbel*

Magazine, September 6, 2019, https://www.babbel.com/en/magazine/the-10 -most-spoken-languages-in-the-world.

Chapter 2

1. The first three divergences are historical facts and so will remain valid over time. The other four divergences will likely continue into the future, but many variables may change the outcome of these narratives over time.

2. Based on chart 17 of ATS "Graduating Student Questionnaire, 2017–2018," with twenty-five respondents as of June 27, 2018. The next two on the list are as follows: interactions with students and experiences in ministry.

3. David H. Kelsey, *Between Athens and Berlin: The Theological Education Debate* (Grand Rapids: Eerdmans, 1993), 6–22.

4. Kelsey, *Between Athens and Berlin*, 18.

5. Jin Li, *Cultural Foundations of Learning: East and West* (Cambridge: Cambridge University Press, 2012), 20–21, 108–23.

6. The quotations from Aleshire are based on the draft manuscript of his work for this series, *Beyond Profession: The Next Future of Theological Education* (Grand Rapids: Eerdmans, 2021).

7. See Strategic Information Report (SIR) of Logos Evangelical Seminary 2019–2020 by ATS, chap. 1, figure 1-15, "Head Count Enrollment." For more details about the design of SIR, see https://www.ats.edu/resources /institutional-data/strategic-information-report.

8. SIR 2018–2019, figure 4-4a.

9. SIR 2019–2020, figure 4-4a.

10. Ted A. Smith, "Model M and Its Afterlives," Currie Lecture, Austin Presbyterian Theological Seminary, January 31, 2017, https://austinsemi narydigital.org/items/show/1159.

11. SIR 2019–2020, figure 7-2b.

12. "Confucian Views and Traditions regarding Women," Facts and Details, accessed February 24, 2020, http://factsanddetails.com/china/cat3 /sub9/entry-5562.html.

13. Jo Ann Deasy, "Data from the Economic Challenges Facing Future Ministers Initiative," based on ATS "Graduating Student Questionnaire, 2016–2017."

14. Based on ATS "Graduating Student Questionnaire, 2015–2016," with thirty respondents.

15. Logos Evangelical Seminary was among the top twenty-five most af-

fordable seminaries in the United States in 2016. "Top 25 Most-Affordable Seminaries, 2016," College and Seminary.com, August 21, 2015, http://college andseminary.com/seminary/the-25-most-affordable-seminaries-in-2015/.

16. M. Thomas Thangaraj, "A Formula for Contextual Theology: Local + Global = Contextual," in *Contextualizing Theological Education*, ed. Theodore Brelsford and P. Alice Rogers (Cleveland, OH: Pilgrim, 2008), 98–107.

17. Chloe Sun, "Reading Job as a Chinese Diasporian," in *T&T Clark Handbook of Asian American Biblical Hermeneutics*, ed. Uriah Y. Kim and Sang Ai Yang (London: T&T Clark, 2019), 295–305.

18. Ekron Chen, "A Richer Mix: Diversity in Logos Evangelical Seminary," in *Logos, Marching Forward! Celebrating Logos' 20th Anniversary*, ed. Andrew Su (Taipei, Taiwan: Grace Publishing House, 2009), 80–81.

19. TOEFL is short for the "Test of English as a Foreign Language."

20. Chen, "A Richer Mix," 83–84, slightly adapted.

Chapter 3

1. Daniel O. Aleshire, "Gifts Differing: The Educational Value of Race and Ethnicity," *Theological Education* 45, no. 1 (2009): 1.

2. For example, Allen P. Ross, "Studies in the Book of Genesis: Pt 3, The Table of Nations in Gen 10—Its Content; Pt. 4, The Dispersion of the Nations in Gen 11:1–9," *Bibliotheca Sacra* 138, no. 550 (1981): 119–38; Eugene H. Merrill, "The Peoples of the Old Testament according to Genesis 10," *Bibliotheca Sacra* 154, no. 613 (1997): 3–22.

3. For example, Bernhard W. Anderson, "Unity and Diversity in God's Creation: A Study of the Babel Story," *Currents in Theology and Mission* 5, no. 2 (1978): 69–81.

4. For example, Eleazar S. Fernandez, "From Babel to Pentecost: Finding a Home in the Belly of the Empire," *Semeia* 90 (2002): 29–50; Hinne Wagenaar, "Babel, Jerusalem and Kumba: Missiological Reflections on Genesis 11:1–9 and Acts 2:1–13," *International Review of Mission* 92, no. 366 (2003): 406–21.

5. For example, Neal Blough, "From the Tower of Babel to the Peace of Jesus Christ: Christological, Ecclesiological and Missiological Foundations for Peacemaking," *Mennonite Quarterly Review* 76, no. 1 (2002): 7–33; David Smith, "What Hope after Babel? Diversity and Community in Gen 11:1–9; Exod 1:1–14; Zeph 3:1–13 and Acts 2:1–3," *Horizons in Biblical Theology* 18, no. 2 (1996): 169–91.

6. For example, John T. Strong, "Shattering the Image of God: A Response to Theodore Hiebert's Interpretation of the Story of the Tower of Babel," *Journal of Biblical Literature* 127, no. 4 (2008): 625–34.

7. "Qin Dynasty," *Wikipedia*, last edited February 22, 2020, https://en.wiki pedia.org/wiki/Qin_dynasty.

8. In Hebrew, the word "name" and the name "Shem" are one and the same.

9. Ekaputra Tupamahu, "Contesting Language(s): Heteroglossia and the Politics of Language in the Corinthian Church" (PhD diss., Vanderbilt University, 2018), ii.

10. J. I. Packer, *Knowing God*, twentieth anniversary ed. (Downers Grove, IL: InterVarsity, 1993), 23.

11. R. W. L. Moberly, *The Theology of the Book of Genesis*, Old Testament Theology (New York: Cambridge University Press, 2009), 141–56.

12. Christopher J. H. Wright, *The Mission of God: Unlocking the Bible's Grand Narrative* (Downers Grove, IL: InterVarsity, 2006), 194–221.

13. Willie James Jennings, *Acts: A Theological Commentary on the Bible* (Louisville: Westminster John Knox, 2017), 27.

14. Jennings, *Acts*, 28.

15. Jennings, *Acts*, 28.

16. G. K. Beale, *The Temple and the Church's Mission: A Biblical Theology of the Dwelling Place of God* (Downers Grove, IL: InterVarsity, 2004), 201. Bock suggests that the list highlights the key communities where the diasporic Jews gathered, which also suggests the global nature of the gospel. See Darrell L. Bock, *Acts: Baker Exegetical Commentary on the New Testament* (Grand Rapids: Baker Academic, 2007), 103.

17. Beale, *The Temple and the Church's Mission*, 202.

18. Bock, *Acts*, 97.

19. Beale, *The Temple and the Church's Mission*, 202.

20. Jennings, *Acts*, 4–5.

21. Jennings, *Acts*, 30.

22. Amos Yong, *The Future of Evangelical Theology: Soundings from the Asian American Diaspora* (Downers Grove, IL: IVP Academic, 2014), 136.

23. Yong, *Future of Evangelical Theology*, 137. Yong articulates the relationship between Spirit and Christ as pneumatology, and this provides the orienting dynamic of Christianity and Christology its thematic focus. Amos Yong, *The Spirit Poured Out on All Flesh: Pentecostalism and the Possibility of Global Theology* (Grand Rapids: Baker Academic, 2005), 28.

24. "Heaven and earth" in the Old Testament sometimes refers to Jerusa-

lem or its temple (Isa. 65:17–18). See Beale, *The Temple and the Church's Mission*, 368. See also J. Richard Middleton, *A New Heaven and a New Earth: Reclaiming Biblical Eschatology* (Grand Rapids: Baker Academic, 2014), 46–48.

25. A YouTube link to the song is https://www.youtube.com/watch?v=SQ_lyaBwxbo.

26. Aleshire, "Gifts Differing," 6.

Chapter 4

1. Douglas McConnell, "Evangelicals, Mission, and Multifaith Education," in *Disruption and Hope: Religious Traditions and the Future of Theological Education, Essays in Honor of Daniel O. Aleshire* (Waco, TX: Baylor University Press, 2019), 101.

2. From the draft of Mark Young's book in this series.

3. https://www.familyfriendpoems.com/poem/human-family-by-maya-angelou.

4. Willie James Jennings, "The Change We Need: Race and Ethnicity in Theological Education," *Theological Education* 49, no. 1 (2014): 35–42.

5. Jennings, "The Change We Need," 37.

6. Jennings, "The Change We Need," 38.

7. Jennings, "The Change We Need," 41.

8. Tod Bolsinger, *Canoeing the Mountains: Christian Leadership in Uncharted Territory* (Downers Grove, IL: IVP, 2015), 43.

Illustrated by Tommy Stubbs

A Random House PICTUREBACK® Book

Random House New York

Thomas the Tank Engine & Friends™

CREATED BY BRITT ALLCROFT

Based on The Railway Series by The Reverend W Awdry.

© 2011 Gullane (Thomas) LLC.
Thomas the Tank Engine & Friends and Thomas & Friends are trademarks of Gullane (Thomas) Limited.
HIT and the HIT Entertainment logo are trademarks of HIT Entertainment Limited.
All rights reserved. Published in the United States by Random House Children's Books, a division of Random House, Inc.,
1745 Broadway, New York, NY 10019, and in Canada by Random House of Canada Limited, Toronto. Pictureback,
Random House, and the Random House colophon are registered trademarks of Random House, Inc.

ISBN: 978-0-375-86799-6

www.randomhouse.com/kids   www.thomasandfriends.com

Printed in the United States of America   10 9 8 7 6 5 4 3 2

The sky over the Island of Sodor was usually calm and blue. But one day, as Thomas and Percy were enjoying a ride in the countryside, they saw black clouds of smoke. They knew there was a fire, and they raced to help.

An old farm shed was in flames. Thomas and Percy let
the farmhands take buckets of water from their tanks.
Luckily, a new engine named Belle arrived. She could shoot
water from her tanks. The flames fizzled and went out.

Everybody agreed that Belle was a Really Useful Engine. Belle
was happy to help, but she knew Sodor needed a real fire engine.
"You need Flynn the Fire Engine. He's a real hero!" she peeped.
Sir Topham Hatt thought this was an excellent idea.

The next day, Thomas took Belle on a tour of the Island of Sodor. They visited Brendam Docks, Knapford Station, and Thomas' Branch Line. Belle liked everything she saw.

Thomas and Belle didn't ask Percy to go with them on the tour. Diesel noticed that Percy was lonely and slid up next to him.

"Thomas is very busy with that new blue engine," Diesel hissed. He invited Percy to visit the Dieselworks.

Percy wasn't sure he should go to the Dieselworks.
Thomas always said Steamies shouldn't puff there—
but Thomas didn't seem to care about Percy lately.
Percy slowly rolled to the Dieselworks. His axles tingled.

"Hello, Percy!" boomed Diesel 10. "What an honor. Please come in."
The Dieselworks was dark, grimy, and a little scary, but the engines
were all very nice, especially Den and Dart. They fixed the Diesels, but
they didn't even have a crane!

"You should tell Sir Topham Hatt you need a new Dieselworks," puffed Percy.

"He doesn't listen to Diesels," said Diesel 10.

Percy had an idea. "I'll ask Thomas to tell Sir Topham Hatt. He always listens to Thomas."

Diesel 10 smiled.

When Percy returned to the Steamworks, he saw that Flynn the Fire Engine had arrived. Everyone was impressed by Flynn because he was bold and red and shiny. Percy felt very unimportant indeed.

Only Kevin listened to Percy's story. Kevin couldn't believe the Dieselworks didn't have a crane.

"Kevin, if you were there, you'd be a hero," Percy puffed. Kevin liked the idea of being a hero very much.

That night, when Percy returned to Tidmouth Sheds, he saw something that made his boiler bubble—Flynn was in *his* berth!

"If I'm not wanted here," Percy thought, "I'll go someplace where they do like me."

Percy found Kevin, and together they rolled to the Dieselworks. They stayed there all night—something no Steamie had ever done before.

Back at the Steamworks the next day, Percy told the steam
engines where he had been. Everyone was shocked. Thomas'
firebox fizzled.

Victor was angry that Kevin was still at the Dieselworks.
He rattled off to tell Sir Topham Hatt.

Percy and Thomas raced to the Dieselworks. Thomas said he would help them get a new building. But Diesel 10 wasn't interested.

"Since Victor isn't at the Steamworks, we're going to take it over—and we want you to lead us, Percy!"

Percy proudly led the Diesels to the Steamworks, but when they got there, no one listened to him.

"The Steamworks is ours," roared Diesel 10. "And we're not giving it back!"

Worst of all, Diesel 10 said Thomas was being held prisoner at the Dieselworks.

Percy knew he'd made a terrible mistake. He quickly went back to the Dieselworks, where Den and Dart were holding Thomas. As Percy screeched to a stop, sparks from his wheels started a fire! Now he had to save Thomas *and* put out a fire!

Percy knew only that one engine could help him now. He raced to find Flynn the Fire Engine. Percy found him at the Sodor Search and Rescue Center. With pistons pumping, the two engines puffed to save Thomas.

At the Dieselworks, Percy convinced Den and Dart to release Thomas. All the engines watched as Flynn boldly pumped water onto the fire.

"Hooray for Flynn!" Thomas peeped.

"He's a real hero," Percy puffed.

The flames hissed and shrank and sputtered out.

Thomas and Percy collected all the Steamies and hurried to save the Steamworks. The Diesels refused to leave.

"Taking things and using trickery is wrong," Thomas peeped. "We can help you get a new Dieselworks, but you have to be fair with us."

Suddenly, Sir Topham Hatt arrived. He was very cross.
"Diesel 10," he said sternly. "You have caused confusion
and delay. Because of you, none of my engines has been
Really Useful."

Diesel 10 whimpered and his claw crumpled.

Sir Topham Hatt explained that the Diesels would get a new Dieselworks. "That was always my plan. Everything takes time. And everyone must wait their turn."

The Diesels and the Steamies agreed to work together to build the new Dieselworks.

When the new Dieselworks was completed, all the engines came together for the grand opening.

Sir Topham Hatt was very proud. "The new Dieselworks shows what can happen when all kinds of Really Useful engines work together," he said.

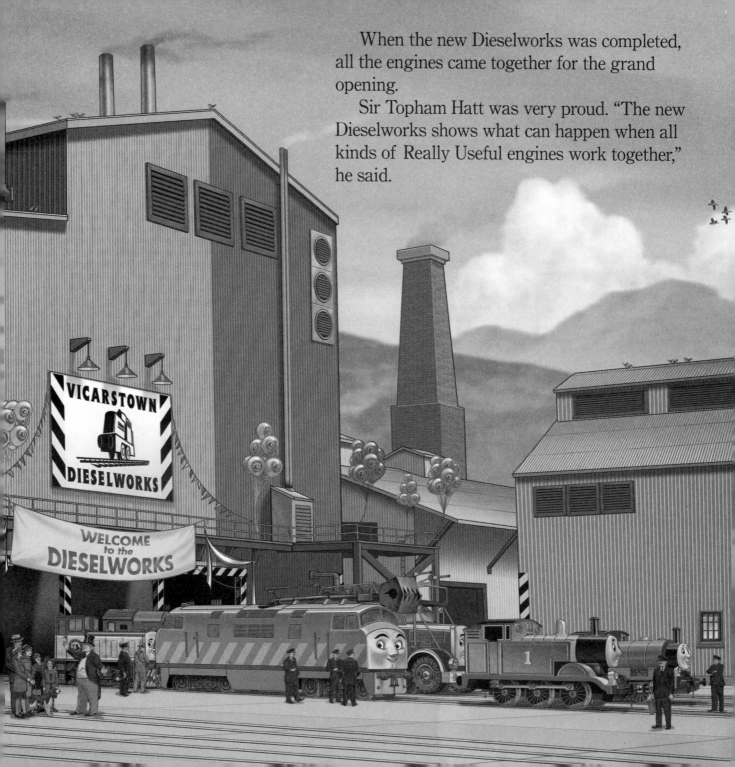

Everyone cheered and all the engines peeped proudly.
Percy and Thomas were especially happy. They were glad to
be best friends again. They giggled and jiggled and puffed
with joy.